FORGIVENESS...

THE RWANDAN WAY

FORGIVENESS...

THE RWANDAN WAY

FRANCINE UMUTESI

authorHOUSE®

AuthorHouse™
1663 Liberty Drive
Bloomington, IN 47403
www.authorhouse.com
Phone: 1-800-839-8640

Published by AuthorHouse   03/05/2015

ISBN: 978-1-4969-0455-3 (sc)
ISBN: 978-1-4969-0456-0 (e)

Library of Congress Control Number: 2014906967

DEDICATION

To Uwintwali Patrick, gone too soon before I could love and appreciate him.

To Munyankindi François-Xavier, the best dad I could ever have asked for . . . it was an honor and privilege to be your daughter. You are missed everyday!

To Mukantagara Goreth, Kanamugire Edouard, Munyaruganda Eurad, Martin, Kimenyi, Kimonyo, Saverina, Tamari Athanasie, Mbonyimbuga Joseph, Yaramutse Beatrice . . . to my grandparents, my cousins, their friends and their families, all my extended family not mentioned, to all the victims of the genocide against Tutsi. You were robbed of life too soon, but you still are and always will be loved; REMEMBERED!

"We did not only lose one million people, we nearly lost the whole country. There was nothing left, no money, no infrastructure. People were left with no families. Today, Rwandans work together, learn from our mistakes and move forward together."

—President Kagame speaking to students and faculty at Stanford University.

"I have always imagined that Paradise will be a kind of library."

—Jorge Luis Borges

"A great book should leave you with many experiences, and slightly exhausted at the end. You live several lives while reading."

—William Styron, Conversations with William Styron

PREAMBLE

This is a forgiveness story.

It is not only my forgiveness story, it is the story of a population—of a nation—that learned to forgive the unforgivable, to tolerate the intolerable, to accept the unacceptable, and to live despite everything.

It is the story of Rwandans!

No science or religion can begin to comprehend what happened in Rwanda before, during, and after the 1994 Tutsi Genocide.

Once you have read my account to the end, only then will you understand why this couldn't have remained in my head, or in my heart.

It is worth putting out there, so that those with eyes can see, and those with a mind can understand what forgiveness really is!

I am not talking about forgiving some trespasses, or forgiving someone who murdered *one* of your loved ones.

I am talking about forgiving somebody who killed ALL your loved ones: your grand-parents, your parents, your cousins, your brothers and sisters . . . somebody who made you an orphan, and who made your country famous by committing Genocide.

I am talking about forgiveness like it has never occurred before!

Lots of Rwandans have no family members and relatives left, many of us because our own have been massacred for their birthright.

Others have their loved ones locked away in prisons, because they became monsters and ignored their humanity for a certain amount of time.

Unlike other genocides and mass murders, the killers were not from a different country, a different background, or even from a different continent.

The Rwandan Genocide was committed by Rwandans against Rwandans, parents against their own children, partners against their partners, and children against one of their own parents . . . and after the Genocide, mostly because there was no other country they could go to, the survivors and the perpetrators were obliged to live in the same country; Rwanda.

They had to face each other. One can only imagine the impulse the survivors felt for vengeance, the impulse the perpetrators felt by seeing that their mission "to kill them all" had failed . . .

And the feeling they both got when they realized
that they had to live together; one can only
speculate as to what they thought when they were
told to live together as one.

Right after this tragedy, survivors and perpetrators
were called to live together and they managed to
achieve this in a really short time. How did this
happen?

Many other Rwandans joined them, coming from
all over the world, from wherever they had lived as
refugees, stateless, as less than nothing.

I with my family came back to Rwanda, hoping to
see our relatives that had remained there, to find
only destroyed houses, and deserted lands full of
cadavers and flowing with blood.

But there was no other choice; we all had to live
together.

It's not like some of us could just take off and go
back to our country, or to any other country for that
matter . . . Finally, we all were in our country.

This Genocide had destroyed a country, yet this
tortured land belonged to us all and whether we
liked or not, we had to learn to share it.

From then on, it was clear that even though
forgiveness seemed impossible for everyone, it was
the only thing that could hold us all together . . . it

was the only way that we could be convinced to tolerate each other.

Although forgiveness was given in many circles, one can't but wonder, does this mean that it was a 100% forgiveness or just tolerance and understanding for everybody's sake?

You will be the judge of that.

The only solution to all Rwandans being to agree that RWANDA as a country belonged to them all with no exception; people accepted the un-acceptable, understood the un-understandable, tolerated the un-tolerable and learned to trust in each other again.

When you read this book, you will finally understand how much human beings are capable of.

How much it can take to be weak, and how little it can take to be strong when one decides to move on; but mostly how much, when you have no other option but to respect justice and life itself, you can accomplish wonders.

This Forgiveness story tells about the strength of a population, the survival and resurrection of a nation.

It starts a long time ago, before my parents were born, before they left and went into exile.

It is a story of more than one lifetime. It is a story of many generations.

By writing this story, I hope my kids will understand more why they don't have as many aunts, uncles, cousins, or second grand-parents as their class mates.

I hope to look them in the eye and tell them "to not ever let this happen to anybody again. To fight for the freedom of all Rwandans, and to never let petty things separate them from their friends whoever they might be!", and hope that they hear me!

Because; this genocide was truly a horrible thing to happen to Rwandans, and it was a terrible thing to happen to the whole humanity.

And it certainly did not benefit the perpetrators or their helpers, nor did it give them any kind of satisfaction.

It made them miserable and imprisoned, and now they are despised by their own people, their own family members!

Worse, it made a whole lot of people orphans!

I know it made my parents brother less, sister less, and orphans forever!

CHAPTER 1

When I was a little girl, I was the daughter of refugees. My family had been in exile for years. I was born in exile, and I only visited my birth country, Rwanda, for the first time when I was seven years old. This situation was not easy for my parents, or for us kids.

After spending many months running and hiding in forests and mountains, my dad had reached his country of exile, Burundi, in 1973, where he tried as best he could to build a life.

The first thing he did was to find a way to survive. He got involved in some businesses, tried to sell whatever he could find before he got a chance to go back to school; he was just in his twenties.

Before fleeing his country, he was training to become a policeman in Rwanda. This was one of the few professions, along with the priesthood and some few others that Tutsis people were allowed to pursue. The rest were only for the Hutus, who at that time were considered to be the elite.

So when the opportunity presented itself in Burundi, when he got the chance, he went for it. One of the programs available at that time in the medical field was the Medical Technician study program. He finished his studies in 1978, and began practicing medicine as a general physician in the province of Kirundo, in northern Burundi.

He met our mom, who had just migrated to Burundi through the Northern Province Kirundo. They knew each other before, because they came from the same place, Kibuye. They then got married and had us, 7 children.

I was born in 1981 as their second child. My older sister Ally and I, being only a year apart, we grew up as twin sisters. We were inseparable!!! And I still like to think that despite the distance that is sometimes between us as I live abroad, we still are!

Growing up, I used to think that my dad was the closest human being to God himself, or at least that when they say at church that all humans are children of God, that my father must have been loved by God a little bit more than others, in order to possess such healing powers.

I even secretly thought my mom to be a bad person, because she was the one who always told us what to do, always punished us, or forbade us to do things we wanted such as disapproving of us when we would banish all beans and vegetables from our plates and preferred eating only rice, fries and meat, like forbidding us to play the whole day with our friends and telling us to wash ourselves twice a day . . . she was a classic, watchful and very loving mother! At home and at school, she was always watching.

She was always busy telling us what to do and what not to do, what's good or bad.

And we had our dad to whom we would tell our misfortunes while sitting on his laps, every time he would get home from work. And he would listen as seriously as he could be with such petty misfortunes and would tell us that he would talk to our mom; and that everything would be ok.

I remember that only then would I feel better, comforted and safe.

Whatever the mistakes we made, we loved him because he would try to talk to us about them, before he would punish us. Our mom on the other hand, was quick to punish us.

Well this shaped us into the law-abiding and respectful human beings that we are today; but right then and there, we didn't understand why.

Having my own kids now, I understand how much she loved us and wanted us to grow into healthy, responsible and disciplined men and women. She was only taking care of our education.

Anyway, in all this, I would always see my dad as my savior, and my rock.

He was a medical doctor, *a great doctor*, and a pious person. He cured almost everybody who came to him, and even when he couldn't cure their illness, obviously medicine and medical doctors are not almighty and they can't cure everything, he would cure their hearts and boost them by supporting them morally, materially, and financially.

Whatever necessary!

I remember that on Sundays, right after the 10am mass, people used to come to our house a lot; some to bring crops from their lands as a thanks gesture for the health care given free of charge, some to bring a private matter for my dad or for my mom to solve/help, and others to ask for some food.

All of these people left always home happy and satisfied. You see, our city having a population of about 300 people, it was easy for him to know them by name, individually.

I felt secure whenever he was around. And because he cured sickness, helped the poor and owned more than one house in our city, I was pretty sure that we were rich and powerful, and that, no matter what, life would go on like that: with only happy events, happy moments, and a happy big family of seven kids, together with my parents, cousins, and friends.

I used to think that he was the protector of the society, or at least the protector of our small city, Gasura!!!

Those were my years of youth and innocence . . .

That period of my life came to an abrupt end when we heard in April of 1994 that all of our relatives and friends living in Rwanda had been killed, that all Rwandans from the Tutsi group had been exterminated, and that my dad's relatives, as well as my mom's, were no more. All of my cousins that I had met in 1988 were dead . . . massacred.

I felt so helpless! I realized that not only all of our family members and friends living in Rwanda were dead, but that my dad couldn't do anything about it.

I had come to believe that he could stop any kind of catastrophe; I believed that he could cure all kinds of sicknesses; I believed that he could protect us from all evil . . .

But not only was he powerless, he was in pain. He was hurting, my mom was hurting, there was only sadness in our home, *and there was nothing he could do about it.*

There was nothing anybody could do about it!

That day, I learned the real meaning of life and death. For the first time in my life, people I knew had died, including my young brother!

That day, I lost what was left of my childhood innocence. I learned that life is what it really is: "A circle of events that starts with the birth of a life, lots of joy and celebrations of this life, and ends with the loss of this same life."

I learned that everybody lived to die someday. That we must never take life for granted, because death awaits us, and that nothing or nobody, not even the Almighty God can prevent us from dying when our time is up.

I understood the meaning of the word "mortal".

I learned about the Circle of Life.

I wanted to be there for my mom and dad; I wanted to be there for my brothers and sisters. Even though I was only 13, I swore that day that in the future I would do my best to help my dad and mom protect the few family members we had left. From that day forward, I swore to be a big girl, to be the big sister to my little brothers and sisters, to be always responsible.

I am not sure if I succeeded to my mission, but I've tried my best since.

To do so, I had to start understanding why we were refugees in the first place, why we were away from our country, and why there was a war in Rwanda. I needed to know what it really meant to be part of Batutsi, Bahutu or Batwa.

I started asking questions, because I couldn't understand why neighbors and friends would start killing each other. I wanted to understand why my brother had died, along with all of my cousins, aunts, uncles, and grandparents!

I don't pretend to have all the answers now, but I will do my best to tell you my story as I lived it and as I learned it.

To help you understand what will follow, there are some things you should know about my country. It will feel like a history class, but believe me, without these details, you would never begin to comprehend what happened to my family, to my relatives, to all Rwandans in general.

You will understand more about my reasons for writing about forgiveness, and tolerance. You will understand how much humanity is capable of, both the worst and the best at the same time!

You have to understand though, Rwanda as a country has a long history, or might I say many versions of history.

Thus far, the final and official version as per the Rwandan people through our politologists is yet to be confirmed and published. They are still trying to straighten up the facts!

Rwandans as well as many Africans have always often used the traditional way of storytelling to pass on their history, their lifestyle.

The way I was taught, and the way I understood and believe my country's history is as follows:

CHAPTER 2

Rwandan history is better understood, when one goes deeper and farther as he can. Only then can one really grasp the real impact of what happened.

Before Colonization[1]

The human presence in Rwanda is thought to have begun shortly after the last ice age, either in the Neolithic period about ten thousand years ago, or in the long wet period that followed, up to about 3000 BC.

The proof is that the archaeological excavations have revealed the dispersal of hunter-gatherers in the late Stone Age, followed by traces of a civilization expert in iron and pottery.

These first inhabitants were the ancestors of Batwa, a group of indigenous Pygmy hunter-gatherers found until now in Rwanda and its neighboring countries.

Between 700 BC and 1500 AD, a number of Bantu groups migrated to Rwanda and began to clear forests for agriculture. The forest was the territory of the Batwa; many lost their homes and were forced to move up the mountain slopes.

Historians have several theories concerning the nature of migration of the Bantu people.

---

[1]   http://www.gov.rw/, My childhood stories, Unity and Reconciliation courses.

One theory is that the first settlers were Hutus, with Tutsis migrating later and forming a distinct ethnic group, possibly Cushitic origin.

Another theory is that migration has been slow and steady, with groups seeking to integrate with, rather than to conquer the existing society.

According to this theory, the distinction between Bahutu and Batutsi emerged later and was a distinction of class as opposed to ethnic group.

In my belief, opinion and experience, the second theory seems more likely, as it has been the case for many known civilizations. And through the historical facts that will follow, you will get your own idea about which of these 2 theories is more likely.

Anyway, history tells us that the first form of social organization in the region was the clan "ubwoko". About 20 clans existed in the Great Lakes Region, the region of East Africa that includes Rwanda. These included:

1.   Abanyiginya
2.   Abasindi
3.   Abatsobe
4.   Abagesera
5.   Abasinga
6.   Abungura
7.   Abahinda
8.   Abahondogo
9.   Abasita

10. Abashambo
11. Abarihira
12. Abongera
13. Abega
14. Abanyakarama
15. Abakono
16. Abacyaba
17. Ababanda
18. Abazigaba
19. Abenengwe
20. . . .

The clans were not limited by family trees, lineages or geographical area, and most included Hutus, Tutsis and Twas.

During the 15th century, the clans began to organize themselves into small kingdoms.

In 1700, about eight kingdoms existed in what is now Rwanda, the largest being Bugesera, Gisaka, the Kingdom of Burundi in the northern part of the actual Burundi, and the early Kingdom of Rwanda.

The Kingdom of Rwanda was ruled by the dynasty Nyiginya and they became increasingly dominant in the mid-eighteen century.

Although some Hutus were among the nobility and significant intermingling took place, the majority made up 82-85% of the population were mostly laborers.

In general, the kings, known as Mwami (translation of King), were from the Tutsis of the clan Abanyiginya.

Before the nineteenth century, it was believed that the Tutsis held military power, and were pastors, owners of herds of cows, while the Hutus owned and took care of lands, and also possessed supernatural powers. In this capacity, the Mwami's council of advisors (*abiiru*) was exclusively Hutus and held significant sway.

As the Kings centralized their power and expanded their Kingdoms militarily, taking control of several small kingdoms, the Kingdom of Rwanda reached its zenith in the nineteenth century during the reign of King Kigeli RWABUGIRI.

King Rwabugiri, after conquering a number of small states and extending the Kingdom to the west on the shores of Lake Kivu and north into what is now Uganda, instigated administrative reforms: the Ubuhake system which included a patronage of cattle for few Hutus who had privileged status.

All these changes created by King Rwabugiri defined the differences between Hutus and Tutsis grups, *differences that were purely social.*

The Twas were basically unaffected, working the land and making pottery as before, with some of them being given the opportunity to become dancers in the royal court. But their numbers continued to decline, as their lives were adapting to changes.

It is said that King Rwabugiri never bothered to assess the ethnic identities of conquered people; he simply labeled all of them "Bahutu."

The labels "Bahutu" and "Batutsi," therefore, *were considered trans-ethnic identities* associated *with socioeconomic, as opposed to ethnic distinctions*.

In fact, one could *"kwihutura,"** or "shed Hutuness," by accumulating wealth and rising through the social hierarchy, becoming a Tutsi.

Under King Rwabugiri, Rwanda became an expansionist state. The Kingdom of Rwanda functioned like any other kingdom. Some European colonialists even talked about the system that was used back then as highly advanced for such "an ignorant people."

The only difference between this kingdom and the others was that it was a small kingdom situated in Africa, and, as such, wasn't worth considering or respecting.

Better yet, it was worth studying, manipulating for the sake of observation, and perhaps even copying; and then destroying as they saw fit.

The kingdom of Rwanda became gradually overwhelmed by European colonial interests starting in 1890. It ceased to exist in 1962 when Rwanda became a republic.

CHAPTER 3

The colonization[2]

A soon as colonialists arrived in the region, they saw that Burundi and Rwanda had similarities especially with their languages that are more than 50% the same. They saw them as one country, hence their appellation: Ruanda-Urundi (actual countries Rwanda and Burundi).

They were also small territories, their own boarders did not count.

The Berlin conference of 1884 delegated the territory known as Ruanda-Urundi to Germany, after drawing boarders without considering the sovereignty of the small kingdoms that already existed, without even recognizing the work and the battles that had been conducted to earn those territories.

This was done to all the countries of Africa. Europeans divided Africa among themselves, and Africans couldn't and still don't have nothing to say or to do about it.

This marked the beginning of the colonial era in this region. Together with the German territory of

---

[2] http://www.gov.rw/, and Wikipedia (edited), My childhood real stories

Tanganyika, Ruanda-Urundi formed German East Africa.

The explorer Gustav Adolf Von Götzen, who later became governor of German East Africa, was the first European to extensively explore the country, in 1894. He crossed to the southeast of Lake Kivu and met the King.

Rwandans being curious and peaceful people welcomed him without hostility.

In Germany, they appointment a resident for Ruanda in 1907. German missionaries and soldiers began arriving in the country shortly thereafter.
The Germans did not significantly alter the societal structure of the country, but exerted an influence by supporting the King and the existing hierarchy, and placing councilors in the courts of local leaders.

In 1919, after the end of World War I and the defeat of Germany, the League of Nations declared Ruanda a mandated territory under the control of Belgium.

The involvement of Belgium was much more direct than that of Germany: they introduces=d large-scale projects in education, health, public functions and agriculture extension.

The Belgians intended the colony to be profitable. They introduced new crops such as coffee as a new commodity crop and used a system of forced labor to have it cultivated.

As the population increased, and with the introduction of new crops that were for export and not for consummation for the local population, they failed to avoid the Ruzagayura famine of 1943-1944*, which killed one-third of the population of Rwanda.

Belgium also maintained the existing class system, emphasizing the promotion of the Tutsi King.

Although the Tutsi, Hutus, and Twas were from different lifestyles, different clans and different families, they had lived together as one people.

They exchanged livelihoods, they married each other, and they gave cows to each others as a sign of appreciation, respect, and brotherhood.

They even had a tradition practice known as "Kunywana", which meant that 2 people who mixed their blood or should I say; who shared their blood became brothers for life, despite them being from Hutus, Tutsi or Twas.

They adored their King who was considered as a supreme because the moment the King was crowned; he ceased to be a Tutsi and was just a King for every Rwandan. They lived with each other in symbiotic harmony.

Of course there had been wars to conquer neighboring territories for centuries . . . but they were always fought based on their home territories, and together as Hutus and Tutsis. Never had there been any conflict or war between the Hutus and Tutsis!

But when the Belgian authorities arrived, they started considering Hutus and Tutsis very differently.

The Belgians' rule created more of an ethnic divide between the Tutsi and Hutu, and they supported Tutsi monarchy.

Due to the eugenics movement in Europe and the United States, and the "divide and rule" strategy that Belgians liked to use, the colonial government became concerned with the differences between Hutus and Tutsis.

Scientists were brought to measure skull—and thus, they believed,—brain size. They thought Tutsis to be taller, their skin to be lighter, and their skulls to be bigger.

As a result of this, Europeans started to believe that Tutsis had Caucasian ancestry, and were thus "superior" to Hutus. God forbid that some Africans be intelligent and still be originated from Africa!

The Belgians gave the majority of political control to the Tutsis, and they were the ones to carry out the force labor onto the rest of the population, Hutus and Twas.

In the 1920s, Belgian ethnologists analyzed (measured skulls, etc.) thousands of Rwandans on analogous racial criteria, such as which would be used later by the Nazis*.

In 1931, an ethnic identity was officially mandated and administrative documents systematically detailed each person's "ethnicity". Every Rwandan got an ethnic identity card.

From 1935, "Tutsi", "Hutu" and "Twa" were indicated on every identity card.

A history of Rwanda that justified the existence of these racial distinctions was written.

It said that "No historical, archaeological, or above all linguistic traces have been found to date that confirm this official history of distinctions.

The observed differences between the Batutsi and the Bahutu were about the same as those evident between the different French social classes in the 1950s.

Only the way people nourished themselves explains a large part of the differences: the Batutsi, since they raised cattle, traditionally drank more milk than the Bahutu, who were farmers."

Although it had been previously possible for particularly wealthy Hutus to become honorary Tutsis and for disgraced Tutsis to be called Hutus, identity cards now prevented any further movement between classes.

The fragmenting of Hutus' lands that occurred in the 1920s ordered by the Belgians angered Mwami Yuhi IV, who had hoped to further centralize his power enough to get rid of the colonialists as it was being done in neighboring countries.

So in 1931, plots against the Belgian administration resulted in the Belgians depositing the Mwami Yuhi.

He was replaced by King Mutara III known as Rudahigwa.

They thought him more controllable, because he was still young. But he had an advanced democratic vision: he abolished the forced labor system that had been instigated by Belgians and distributed cattle and land to everyone.

In 1943, he became the first Mwami to convert to Catholicism, and this willingly.

However, because of the existence of many wealthy Hutus who shared the financial, if not physical stature of the Tutsi after this distribution, the Belgians used an expedient method of ethnic classification based on the number of cattle a person owned.

Anyone with ten or more cattle was considered a member of the Tutsi class.

The Roman Catholic Church, the primary educators in the country, subscribed to and reinforced the differences between Hutu and Tutsi. They developed separate educational systems for each, favoring the Tutsi monarchy at first.

Following World War II, Ruanda-Urundi became a trusted territory of the United Nations.

Belgium, just like all the other colonialists, received a mandate to oversee the colonies' independences.

Some of them complied and oversaw in some way, the implementation of the independences in their colonies, though still present in some way.

But the Belgians refused to grant independence to Rwanda.

The King and the Rwandan authorities manly composed of Tutsi wanted to force the freedom from them, but they didn't get the chance.

The Belgians withdrew their longstanding support to the existing Tutsi hierarchy and started promoting the Hutu party.

They started encouraging tensions between the population, showing the Hutus that the Tutsis had oppressed them by being on the power for so long, spreading rumors saying that Tutsis were conquerors that had taken the Hutus' lands, and that they were foreigners.

These tensions became more intense in the 1950s and peaked in 1959.

The King on his way back from a consultation with Belgian Officials, to discuss the independence of his country, died on 25th of July 1959 in Bujumbura, Burundi, after being treated for a headache by a Belgian physician.

Although some people confirm that he died of a cerebral hemorrhage (Book by Rosamond Haley Carr, on a discussion she had with a physician who has examined his body, Dr. David Stewart of Louisville, Kentuchy), this was purely and simply an assassination.

Thinking about the circumstances of his death, what would you think?

A party named PARMEHUTU "The party of the Hutu Emancipation Movement" was founded by Gregoire Kayibanda. A Hutu Manifesto got written, and it contained commandments of Hutus, detailing how much Hutus should hate Tutsis, and why Tutsi were enemies, and had to die by all means, had to be exterminated!

In 1959, after the death of King Mutara III, Hutus militants started what they called the revolution:

they began killing Tutsis wherever they were causing hundreds and thousands of deaths, burning their houses and forcing almost 2 million to seek refuge abroad.

Between 1961 and 1962, an anti-Tutsi referendum was conducted, and elections in which the country voted the abolition of the monarchy was conducted.

Rwanda was separated from Burundi and obtained its "independence" under Kayibanda in 1962.

This wasn't a deserved independence seeing that it excluded a big part of the Rwandans; it was independence just because it was supported by the colons.

The circles of violence and killings against Tutsis continued during the following years.

In 1973, Juvenal Habyarimana, declaring that the current government had become too corrupt, inefficient, and violent, organized a military coup and assumed the presidency of the Republic of Rwanda. Several high ranking officials were killed, including Kayibanda and his wife.

In the years that followed the coup, Rwanda enjoyed a "relative" economic stability, but discrimination against Tutsis continued. The twas remained marginalized, and in 1990 were almost entirely driven from the forest by the government.

Meanwhile, the Rwandese Alliance for National Unity (RANU) was formed in 1979 by Rwandan refugees in exile, to mobilize against divisive politics and genocide ideology, repeated massacres, statelessness and the lack of peaceful political exchange. In 1987, RANU became the Rwandese Patriotic Front (RPF).

After making several attempts to organize a dialogue with the current government and reaching to nothing, things took another direction.

On the 1st October 1990, the RPF launched an armed liberation struggle that ultimately ousted the dictatorship in 1994 and ended the genocide of more than 1 million Tutsis and massacres of moderate Hutus who opposed the Genocide.

CHAPTER 4

When the RPF attacked Rwanda, they were seeking both to put an end to a regime that was oppressing Tutsis and to establish a new regime based on the unity of all Rwandans: Hutus, Tutsis and Twas. This was the beginning of a war that lasted 4 years.

The Rwandan government, helped by French troops, tried to suppress the RPF, but they regrouped and captured the Northern Territory within 10 days.

Under pressure and with the fear that the RPF could actually win, the government started to consider entering into negotiation with the Rwandans living outside the country. Over the next year and a half, neither side was able to gain a decisive advantage.

Meanwhile, the war weakened the president Habyarimana, and in 1992 demonstrations began en masse, forcing him to enter into coalition with opposition parties and others insisting on seeking peace with the RPF.

Despite continuing violence against Tutsis, except in areas controlled by the RPF, the two main parties agreed to a cease fire in 1993, and began to negotiate a peace agreement under United Nations supervision, in Arusha Tanzania.

Unfortunately, even under the UN supervision, things took an unexpected turn!

President Habyarimana, who was considered to be weak by his supporters because he had agreed to negotiate with the "enemy", was killed in a private plane crash, together with his homologue Burundian, at Kanombe International Airport in Rwanda.

Over the years, his death has been interpreted in many different, though consistently self-serving, ways.

Some people supported by French officials say that the RPF killed him. But when you think about their motives, they make no sense.

For a long time, the RPF and Rwandans abroad had tried to negotiate their return to their country . . . as if one should have to beg in order to go back to his own country . . . in vain. This one guy has finally accepted, even though under pressure, to sit down at the same table with the RPF and listen.

And he was listening, perhaps even inclined to let them come back to Rwanda for the sake of peace. So why would they kill him at a crucial moment when everything seemed possible?

Now the other plausible theory about his death is that his closest friends and family got fed up with his "weakness" and used him for their motive: to create a reason that would convince Hutus to participate en mass to the genocide that they had planned, advocating that they should take revenge over Tutsis for killing their president. And this is plausible because it actually worked.

More than 1,000,000 Tutsis and few moderate Hutus who refused to take part in those killings were massacred in a period of 100 days only!!!

In my belief, this second theory is the most plausible because the death of Habyarimana was not only well planned, but it benefited those who committed it by using it and making it an excuse for executing one of the worst Genocide the world has ever seen.

His death marked the beginning of the worst nightmare any Rwandan or any human being had ever lived.

Friends started killing friends, parents their own kids from their Tutsi partners, and kids their own parents.

Hell descended on earth for a 100days!!!

Bottom line; from the colonialism, we did not inherit development, good manners, education, or health facilities . . . *we inherited a Genocide*.

This hatred of Hutus against Tutsi was not created in one day. It was a product of long and hateful teachings made by the authorities since 1950s.

They taught the population from an early age that Tutsis were foreigners who had come to occupy their country centuries ago, that the country belonged to Hutus, and that the others were nothing more than invaders who should be sent back to their countries by any and all means.

And send them back they did: first in 1959, when Tutsi people were hunted, chased from their homes, their lands, and killed them as they fled.

Over the years, neither the chasing nor the killing ever stopped, though for the sake of the international community's opinion, there were some false peace periods. These lulls were short-lived, however, as the violence would inevitably flare up again in response to any political events.

For example, in 1973, when the Hutu president Habyarimana organized a "coup d'état" and took the power, Tutsis were blamed and killed, chased throughout the country.

This was the time my dad fled the country. He was one of the Tutsis who fled during the massacres of 1973, following the coup.

The story of his escape had become a fairytale to my siblings and me, that after hearing it, my sister Clark vowed to be a law officer when she would be of age. In a way, she succeeded since she just graduated from the school of Law and Administration. Our father would be proud of her.

Anyway, let me tell you about how he escaped.

It was an afternoon like any other, when he heard on the radio that President Kayibanda and his family was dead, and that Habyarimana had committed a coup and was now the president.

Knowing very well that any political incident was dangerous and could cost Tutsis lives, he feared the worst. But in order to avoid any suspicions, he continued to act normally with his friends and classmates. He was training to become a policeman.

So, on his way back from the training, he followed his classmates to a bar club, where they usually took a glass of beer before they would go home. He was hoping that by staying close to them, he would learn more about the situation, and perhaps even feel safer.

But as the time to go home approached, they all left without inquiring if he needed anything. And him as proud as he was couldn't ask for help, especially as he didn't know who would help him and who would throw him under the bus.

Anyhow, minutes after they left, he also left the bar.

On his way home, he suddenly realized that he was being followed. He couldn't identify his followers, but they weren't friendly considering the stones they were throwing and the sticks they had at hand.

27

So he began to walk faster, and then to run. He run as fast as he could!

At first, he was going into the direction of his house. But after some reflection, he thought that it might be better to head into a different direction, since others could already be waiting for him there.

You see virtually all Tutsi houses were continuously monitored and known. This was one of the main factors that allowed the Genocide perpetrators of 1994 to do such a "good" job . . . they already knew who to kill, and where to find them.

Anyway, he realized that there was a high probability that his own house would be under surveillance.

He continued to run, and gradually accelerated. Just as he was starting to think that he was out of reach, he heard dogs chasing after him, obviously let loose by his pursuers.

Not knowing what to do, and fearing for his life, he ran and ran, zigzagging . . . and plop . . .

He fell into a hole of at least 6metters deep, one that was destined to become an outside latrine.

It had rained that day, so as you can imagine, the hole was muddy. But fearing for his life, he didn't even breathe or try to come out of it. He was hoping that since it was night and they couldn't see him, the dogs would lose his smell, and would lose him. But they were good. They came right on top of the hole, and they stopped there.

His pursuers then trying to make him come out, started throwing stones into the hole, anything they could get the hands on. But he didn't move.

After what he thought as an eternity, they got tired. Hoping that the stones had killed him, or that as there was no movement the dogs had been mistaken and he was gone, they finally left.

He waited until the following evening to come out, and from there escaped to Burundi. He left behind his parents and siblings who lived in Kibuye. In a way, he was saved by this lowly toilet hole.

Kibuye being a western province with not much interest to the government and a place where lived too may Tutsis for their taste, had been ignored over the years. In addition, it is a mountainous territory, so getting there was difficult.

This was one of the reasons that many aspired to go and study elsewhere, or simply to go and live in Kigali. My dad had moved for the same purpose: get an education or a professional training for his future.

Like many Rwandan Tutsis, he was bind to follow only some particular carriers and trainings allowed to them by the government.

So, after this escape, he understood that there was no future for him in Rwanda, he realized that all Tutsis living in Rwanda would be at some point chased and killed sooner or later . . . so, he had to get used to the idea of living as a refugee in a foreign country, Burundi.

Trying to save as much as he could, he later tried to get members of his family to Burundi for their protection, but he will have only managed to save only 3: his two younger brothers, and one of his many nephews.

It wasn't easy to enter and to exit Rwanda and going back there had many risks: whenever they would catch a Rwandan living abroad in visit to their families, they would execute him, after torturing him/her trying to get information about RANU or the RPF. They believed that everybody was out to get them, that all Rwandans abroad were RPF members, therefore, RPF spies.

As it turns out, if they would have all come to live abroad, they could have been saved . . . but ifs don't make things real.

CHAPTER 5

Well, after so much struggle and hard work in Burundi, my father managed to graduate from a medical school as a Medical Technician. I am not sure to what this degree corresponds nowadays, but he practiced medicine as a general physician since.

He was sent to the northern province of Burundi, known as Kirundo, and this is where he started his family.

We all had a happy childhood. Our parents were "good people". In addition to being a doctor, my dad helped folks with whatever problems they had, whether they be medical, financial, or emotional.

Everyone knew that in order to get better, they could go "kwa Muganga" "at the doctor's" and get whatever was missing.

I grew up in a loving and big family, with three sisters and three brothers. I want you to meet all of them here because I will be referring to them throughout this book.

My big sister Ally, 1 year older than me, was born in 1980. She and I have been like twins since we were little. We started primary school together, because I refused to stay at home alone without her. I was stubborn like that. And probably I still am.

This was the beginning of our many adventures together, at school as well as our everyday life. We passed our classes together and, most of the time, she would be 1st and I would be 2nd, or vice versa. We used to be so close that people actually would think that we were twins . . . even though we're so different . . . she so tall and beautiful; and I, shorter with a lighter skin.

My younger sister Wera, born the year after me, was the calmest and least talkative. She would sit in a corner and watch us fight over nothing, and would only say, 'Stop it, stop it.' Of course that never worked. But when the fight would go towards her, she knew how to defend herself very well. She remains a calm person to this day.

I fought constantly with my little brother Patrick, who was two years younger than I. He was motivated to declare the house his territory, but I was not ready to let him. We all weren't ready to let him, so in return, he fought with everyone!

When I think back, I realize now how much I loved him, but wanted him to accept his role as my baby brother. And that was impossible for him to understand, especially considering that he was the only boy among us—at least at the time. While our dad was at work, and maybe because Patrick felt stronger, he liked to show off.

Unfortunately, I never had time to straighten things out with him, or to be an adult with him, because I lost him far too early; we lost him before we could even understand each other, back in the 1994 massacre that took place in Kibuye, Rwanda. I will never forget him!

I think about him every day, and whenever I see somebody's brother, whenever I see my cousins who have the same age, I wonder what it would feel like if he were still alive.

What it would be like if I had a brother to share everything with, to love, to consult when I am confused, and to help me out when I can't bear the burden of life . . . What if he was around to dry the tears of suffering from our mom's cheeks, now that she is alone and sole head of our family . . . To wash off the tears on all our cheeks. *What if?*

We'll never know, but we'll always miss him!!!

My sister Clark, four years my junior, was so animated that she used to start fights with our brother Patrick, and would end up fighting with all of us at the same time.

She wouldn't rest; sometimes it seemed like in a horror movie, with everybody fighting and crying. But when our mom would ask who started the fight, it would always be Patrick's fault; he being the only boy among us . . . Clark was so energetic, yet so timid.

Sadly, she lost her innocence after witnessing the massacre of our cousins in 1994, at our aunt's house in Butare, where she was living at the time. More about this incident will be explained later.

When our younger brother Ben was born, in 1986, our parents thought that he was our last. Hence, the name Benjamin, but fondly known as Ben. It was obvious that we all needed some peace, some space.

But this was only the birth of another warrior into the family.

Because 4 years later, Fabrice, our last born came along. I remember everything about his birth, his childhood and all. He was our last, and probably the most loved by everyone so far!

The reason to this is probably because we were all a lot older than him and we understood better what it meant to be big sisters and brothers.

Hence the big family I was talking about: our parents had a total of seven kids. Despite the fights I mentioned, which I believe happen in most of big families, we were a happy and loving family.

I remember the fights because, as you must be thinking, or like any child, I was more focused on them than on the lovely times we spent together with our parents.

The happy moments at school when our brother would fearlessly protect his sisters against everybody bigger or smaller than him, or the quiet and loving moments spent sitting in our living room with our parents, or outside under the moon light, listening to old fairytales/stories of ancient Rwanda know as "imigani."

For primary education, we all, except for the younger one Fabulous who never started his school in Burundi, went to a public primary school in Gasura, somewhere in the northern province of Burundi. This was the only primary school in this small town where my dad worked as the Clinic's head doctor.

When my sister Ally and I started primary school, I was only five. My sister was ready to start, as the age for starting was 6, but as I was reluctant to stay home alone, I insisted on coming along.

The school director saw no objection to my starting early. In addition, the school officials figured that if I didn't pass, I would simply retake the class the following year.

But, surprisingly enough, I finished second in the class with my sister being the first. And from there, we continued together until high school.

We all went to the same school, and we were good pupils in order to meet our father's high expectations. I remember him being very serious about our education, and he would help us with our homework every evening.

He had his own system for teaching us. I remember that for example with our French course, he would give us a French book to read and he would beat the hell out of us using his fingers, whenever we were unable to read a word that we had learned before.

His favorite punishment was to "turn in our ears!" After two or three turn-ins, we could read a French textbook better than the French themselves, because it was just too painful to bear, or to risk having another one.

To this day, I'm convinced that this was the best encouragement possible, because this helped us take our French, as well as our other courses seriously.

He also gave us the spirit of competition by putting in place a system of rewards at home: The first one to get good marks was always invited to go to our mom's job place, to order anything he or she likes.

Our mom was the owner of a "Cercle Sportif" "a sort of sport club comprised of a hall for the town meetings and mostly sport clubs meetings, a bar, and a restaurant that focused on grilled goat meat and bananas.

So this was a real reward for a young kid, to go there, sit with the grownups and order a "brochette" of goat with grilled bananas, and a "fanta*" of your choice. We all worked hard to get this opportunity, every trimester.

Our young brothers and sisters did not benefit from this system a lot, because most of the time when their time to go to school arrived, we were moving around, either running from the Burundi insecurities and killings, or later moving back to Rwanda after the Genocide of 1994.

CHAPTER 6

I was ten when we started going to meetings organized by Rwandans living in Burundi. They were called Ibitaramo*: Get-togethers. Officially, their purpose was to keep our Rwandan culture alive through dance, storytelling, proverbs, etc.

But unofficially, they also were a place where everybody came to stay up to date, as to the war that was happening in Rwanda at the time.

This being 1991, RPF had already attacked Rwanda, and progress had been made, but there was still many difficulties, and the promise to go back home was not certain.

Children of course would have their play time, and grownups their update and we would all go home happy and hopeful.

I used to wonder why our neighbors were not like us.

Then I started wondering why they were not coming to those meetings as well, or why there were some differences such as the way our parents spoke with a different accent, that later turned out to be a Rwandan accent; why our ways of living were different from those of our neighbors, especially when it came to the kind of education and traditions; why we weren't as welcome in all the circles of the society even though my dad was the most respected and the most generous person in town, and my mom was loved by everyone and gave favor to whoever needed one.

I would wonder why at school we were always asked more questions than others. Why we had to behave better than the other pupils, because we received more suspensions, and for example, in order to pass the tests in 6th grade required to go on to high school, why we had to score higher than the others by 3 to 5 points.

More was always required of us: with our behavior, our marks, our tiny little moves.

But far from being harmful, these requirements made us stronger. As I grew up, I came to realize that these high standards actually trained us to be better!

So, in those gatherings I started learning a lot. Although it was mostly to have fun, get to know other Rwandan kids, and share with them, dance and play together, we also learned a lot about our country Rwanda, through storytelling and testimonies, as well as teachings.

For example, we started learning the most important thing: that we were Rwandans (not Burundians), and that we should always take pride in that.

But, for safety reasons, we weren't allowed to mention it everywhere or to everyone. Although we were supposed to be proud, we were also supposed to be careful.

Some Rwandans were even ashamed or just afraid to confirm that they were Rwandans, so they took the Burundian nationalities or others nationalities of their host countries just to be able to be treated as human beings.

But for others, they were not ready to abandon their origins, theirs birthrights. They just wanted to be recognized as Rwandans.

So, one thing was clear at that time, but perhaps not entirely to a 10-year-old: "We were Rwandans and should always be proud of it! We were never to show our pride in front of other people, never to mention it to anyone; we had just to learn to blend in with the other kids, unless someone asked us about it. Then we were not to comment and to go straight home and tell our parents."

This probably had something to do with the fact that Burundi shared and still does in a way, the same history as Rwanda throughout the ages; we speak almost the same languages with 90% resemblance of words, we have the same history, same clans, same tribes and same ethnic problems, and at some point during the colonization, both countries were considered to be one country for decades, named: Rwanda-Urundi.

The sole difference resided in the fact that while Hutus of Rwanda were busy killing Tutsis and chasing them out of Rwanda, the King of Burundi decided to get separated to Rwanda, get their own independence, and live peacefully with all their countrymen.

Hutus of Burundi tried to carry out the same treatment to Tutsis as it was happening in Rwanda, but each time, they were unsuccessfully.

And although they didn't have a perfect and secure country where to give asylum, they accepted to receive the Rwandans that were fleeing the killings in their country just like all the other neighboring countries such as Uganda and Zaire (actual Democratic Republic of Congo).

The Burundians also lived many coups d'état, many killings of Hutus against Tutsis and then retaliations from Tutsis against Hutus, and many other inter-ethnic small wars. But Tutsis of Burundi continued to rule, trying to advocate for unity every time.

With all the insecurities, you can imagine how much the peace that we lived in was fragile.

But there was no other choice, right? It's not like we would have just gone back home . . .

We lived in constant fear, in constant wait for the next catastrophe, the next attacks, and the next time we would be called to flee again.

There were many more things that we learned through those gatherings; we learned that our goal was never to stay abroad: "kubaho ishyanga", it was never to stay "stateless"; but to have the chance to go back and live in our own country, with the rest of our families, to have a place to call home.

Then came the time I learned that there were some people who didn't want us to go home, to Rwanda.

Those same people had persecuted our parents and their parents, and that only those who were able to flee had gone abroad, and were now living as refugees like my parents.

I learned then that I was a REFUGEE, and perhaps a stateless person.

It was clear that we had to know and keep one promise in our hearts: no matter how long it took, we would return to our homeland someday.

That we were, and would always be Rwandans, *Proud Rwandans*! And nobody had the right to take it from us!

It was like learning some sort of important news, and hearing of some "promised land" that is somewhere far away, but that will eventually be reached, no matter the wait, no matter the sacrifice.

I took faith in that very much. I had just learned that I was stateless and as devastated as a 10 year old could be, I was devastated!!! But I also had a consolation statement that said that we had a home, and that it was a matter of time before we could go there.

Most of the songs we sang and danced to had lyrics such as, "Rwanda, igihugu cy'amata n'ubuki, gihugu cy'imisozi ibihumbi . . ."

. . . meaning: "Rwanda, the country of milk and honey, the country of a thousand hills . . . !"

Or "Genda Rwanda uri nziza, oh uhumeka amahoro; ibyiza bigutatse Rwanda, ni byinshi cyane, sinabivuga ngo mbirangize . . ."

. . . meaning: "Oh Rwanda you are beautiful, and you breathe peace; the wonders that decorate you Rwanda are too many that I couldn't manage to talk about them all . . ."

. . . and then the song would go on listing the volcanoes, the mountains, the lakes, and the Rwandan people from the time when they were all one people . . .

I remember longing to see it! Wouldn't you? Just like Christians long to see Heaven, I wanted to go see my parents' country, meet again my grandparents, my aunts and uncles and my cousins . . . I just wanted to feel home, and to be finally somewhere I and my family would feel safe.

I thought that it would be automatic. That being in Rwanda meant being home, being safe, and being in a loving environment.

Reaching our country with new leaders and a new strategy of governing as we were being taught: with unity.

These meetings started cultivating unifying ideology that all Rwandans were the same and were supposed to live in their country peacefully, equally and safe.

This was the first time I ever was interested in listening to news with my dad, and I even started asking questions about Rwanda, about our families, about politics, especially Rwandan politics.

But unfortunately, when we finally got to go home, when we finally got to Rwanda after the Genocide, what a horrible spectacle we witnessed!!!

There wasn't so much milk and honey left; there wasn't anything sweet at all . . .

Our family members that we had met in the summer of 1988 when we went to Kibuye for a short visit, our beloved relatives that we all longed to meet had been massacred. There was no beautiful "promised land"; it was all gone—*all destroyed!*

Instead of flowing with milk and honey, the country was flowing with blood, from all over the place, cadavers were lying everywhere, dogs had become wild and attacked even living people just passing by . . . it was a nightmare!!!

I remember this because I witnessed it with my family. We got back to Rwanda on the 4th of August right after the liberation of Kigali city, and until this moment, I wish I could un-see the horrors we saw on the way from Kirundo, to Kigali, passing by Nyamata.

CHAPTER 7

Before 1990s, whenever the topic of letting the Rwandans abroad come back to Rwanda would come up, the Rwandan government, led by President Habyarimana always would give many excuses as to why they cannot let the other Rwandans back into the country.

The most famous was that: "There were not enough space for everyone, first for Rwandans that were in the country. And that those living abroad should remain abroad since they are not even real Rwandans."

To emphasize this statement, many of those who were killed during the Genocide and even before, were mostly thrown into the river called *Nyabarongo*,* which is believed to flow from the source of and into the Nile*.

Their killers would tell them that they were helping them return to their homeland, Abyssinia* (present-day Ethiopia), through a shortcut.

On the 1st of October 1990, when the Rwandan Patriotic Front (RPF)* first attacked Rwanda, my sister and I were in 4th grade. We knew that something was going on right away, and we were worried, of course.

It's important to remind you that the members of
the RPF were Rwandans who had been driven
away from their country, Rwandans who had tried
unsuccessfully to negotiate their peaceful return
home over the years.

Rwandans who had called upon the International
Community since the 1950s, denounced the killings
that were happening, but had been ignored as if
their death meant nothing to anybody . . .

*So, far from being a rebel attack as it was labeled
by many as soon as it started, this was a cry for
justice. A last resort just to say: enough is enough!!!
Let's try and get justice by and for ourselves!*

People were tired of living away from home, and
even though I was young, I remember very well
feeling insecure and uncomfortable all the time.

All the capable men and women got mobilized
to join the front, and many responded. It was
considered an honor to participate in the battle for
the return of everyone home.

Everybody agreed that the years spent abroad were
enough, they didn't want to be called refugees or
beggars anymore, to be treated like nobody, and to
live in constant insecurity.

I remember that my dad's nephew Rukundo, and
one of his brothers Kiza joined the cause as well.

I also remember that when I finally understood what was going on, I regretted not being of age to join. I so much wanted to be part of this wonderful act, this return, whether armed or not.

The others who couldn't join did help otherwise. For example, by sending food stocks to the front, medical supplies, and others things needed at the front.

My dad served like this; he used to take trips once a month or even more than that, as needed, with a truck full of medical and food supplies.

While he was gone, my mom would stay worried until he would get back.

He would go to camps full of Rwandans who had fled killings to Burundi, the famous one being in a small town called Mushiha, and stay to treat people for 1 or 2 weeks before heading back home.

Immediately after the first attack, the mood in the Rwandan communities changed. It was palpable.

We all finally had hope. Anybody could feel it, and the Burundians could feel it as well.

And then, after only few days of fighting, the leader of the RPF, *Late Major Gen. Fred Gisa Rwigema** and some of his closest generals and head of battalions got killed.

This stroked everyone hard! The dream was threatened, and many felt desperate.

Major Gen. Fred Gisa Rwigema was one of the founding members and leader of the RPF Inkotanyi.

He was among the first Rwandans to express the need to get back to Rwanda by all means, hence the creation of the Rwandese Alliance for National Unity (RANU) in 1979, transformed into the Rwandan Patriotic Front (RPF) IN 1987.

The government of Rwanda lead by Habyarimana rejoiced. Everybody was wondering what would happen from there on. The "rebellion" as they called it was weakened, and they believed that all was over.

You see, in lots of African revolutions either against European colonialists or against dictators, leaders had been the main targets, mostly because this meant that if the head is cut, the body most probably won't be able to survive.

And right they were, considering many revolutions that we know throughout history. Look at what happened to Major General SANKARA* of Burkina Faso and his revolution.

So, nobody expected the RPF to stand up again, and to reach such victories in the days that followed.

Francine Umutesi

Lead by the current President of Rwanda (2003-to date), then Major General Paul Kagame who took matters in his hand when everyone was hopeless, they took control of the North-Eastern provinces of the country from the government's army that was backed up by French troops, in a matter of days.

The RPF defeated the government and its supporters, French soldiers miserably. It was a phenomenal victory; the first of many that followed.

Although we were all in mourning, it wasn't long that we started having hoping again, that we started rejoicing.

The current government of Rwanda felt strongly the power of the RPF especially because they had an unshaken will and motivation to return to their homeland.

They felt it because for many years, they had relaxed and believed that if the French government was with them, nobody could touch them.

But this came as a chock to everybody. The French couldn't believe it, the UN finally got their attention picked, and the whole world finally noticed those Tutsis, that minority that had just dared to defeat French troops as well as Rwandans . . .

But they all called it a rebellion; they saw RPF attack as a rebel attack on a sovereign country Rwanda.

For a long time, they went on with this idea, proclaiming that some rebels had attacked Rwanda, everybody wanted to get involved in the protection of Rwanda.

Calls got made by the UN, France, USA . . . and many other countries denouncing the attacks.

But the RPF, knowing that they had to fight for their own freedom and their rights did not flinch.

They had their goal set, and they wanted to return to their country, peacefully or not.

Seeing their unshaken will and strength, somehow the UN, the International Community, the Rwandan government at the time found no other remedy than to start a negotiation process.

They were losing the war, and sooner or later, the president of Rwanda was seeing that he would lose the whole country.

So, whether they were stalling to make new plans, or sincere, the fact is that they agreed to enter negotiations supervised by the United Nations.

Once again, hope struck in the Rwandan communities.

For so long, they had tried to attract the International community's attention on the killings that were happening in Rwanda against Tutsis, to the homeless and stateless Rwandans spread across the globe, and nobody had paid attention.

And only some months of strategic war against Rwanda and its French allies, and the RPF was recognized and even given an ear for negotiation.

The UN finally got involved.

Normally whenever there is a crisis, one expects the UN agencies to be all over the problem, trying to help here and there, and to solve it.

I had never seen an agent of the UN in my life, until after the Genocide, and mostly on TV in refugee camps made of Hutus that had just committed the atrocities in Rwanda.

By saying this, I want to emphasize the fact that the UN had ignored many Rwandan refugees over the years, at least in the place where I grew up, most probably because they had ignored the killings against Tutsis of Rwanda.

Recognizing these refugees would have made it clear that there was a problem in Rwanda.

And recognizing a problem in Rwanda would have obliged them to solve it.

And nobody wanted that! Nobody had the gut to stand up and ask questions, especially not to a country that is a great friend of France.

Some will always wonder why Rwanda was so important to France, myself included.

Until now, I haven't found anybody that can give me a satisfactory explanation. I will never understand why they had to get involved, and help kill millions of people they had no interest killing.

Unless they did, and that, I would love to know!

The fact is that with the support of the countries that make decisions in the UN Security Council like France, Rwanda benefited with the highest protection and there was a certain "laisser faire" from everyone . . . for a long time.

Tutsi had no chance: they were dying, some by the hand of the Hutus inside Rwanda, and others by hunger in refugee camps or poverty in their misfortunate homes abroad, all over the world.

Nobody raised his little finger as to even show that they cared.

CHAPTER 8

I used to think that the war would come to us in Burundi. I would worry day and night. But of course, as I said earlier, I believed that as long as my dad was home, I believed that everything would be all right.

Living in Burundi, we thought that we were far from the front lines, but we were sadly mistaken.

In 1993, presidential elections were held in Burundi, and the elected Hutu president was assassinated only after three months in office. This was followed by "imvururu*"—"the chaos"—during which many Burundian Tutsis were killed. And, as if that weren't enough, Burundian Hutus came after us— Rwandans living in Burundi.

While everybody was fleeing and taking their families to safety, which was the capital city Bujumbura at the time, my kind and generous dad steadfastly refused to leave people in need.

Among these injured people were mainly Tutsis and Hutus injured while killing one another.

He stayed in his clinic, waiting and helping out whoever was injured, without discrimination.

But of course, although he was not ready to leave he made sure that we were safe first, and took us to the capital city of Bujumbura, where security was guaranteed.

We were to stay at our aunt's home until the rest of the country was safe. We ended up living there for almost a year.

Meanwhile, in Rwanda, 1993 was the year when a ceasefire was declared, and a Peace Treaty signed by the government and the RPF Inkotanyi.

President Habyarimana declared that he was ready to listen, ready to negotiate the return of the Rwandans living abroad, and ready to let them participate in the development of their country.

A United Nations peacekeeping force was deployed to Rwanda; the UN put in place a mechanism to assist the negotiations, even placing a UN peace corps in Kigali known as United Nations Assistance Mission for Rwanda (UNAMIR).

To talk about this period is incredibly painful for me, because it is during this ceasefire that people, believing in the changes that were being promised, started making changes in their own lives.

Some of these changes and decisions proved fatal, including ones that led to the loss of my brother, in addition to my whole extended family.

You see, for the first time since 1959, there was hope. Tutsis still living in Rwanda hoped to see their long lost relatives who had fled the country and those abroad were impatient to finally have a place they could call home.

Some refugees even started moving back home from abroad, where they had lived for many years, taking jobs and resettling in their homeland. People who had not seen family members could visit both within Rwanda and across its borders.

Prior to this time, any Tutsi caught either leaving or entering Rwanda was jailed for treason, and sometimes executed, suspected of being a spy for the RPF Inkotanyi.

I remember back in 1988, when I was seven; my mom took my siblings Ally, Clark, Patrick, and me to meet our grandparents. Sadly, this turned out to be our first and only visit.

In order to cross the Burundi-Rwanda border, we had to take some shortcuts through the forest, to avoid highways and custom offices.

This was not to break the law nor to hide from it, but to make sure we stayed alive . . . Two of our uncles Kimenyi and Edouard had come to meet us on the border, in order to help mother with carrying us.

Our dad had to take us to some place at the border of Kirundo and Bugesera, and then they helped us cross and returned with us.

We walked for three days, sleeping along the way. To pick up the pace, they transported us on their backs and shoulders.

But when we reached Kibuye, our parents' hometown, that arduous trip was all worth it. We got to meet our grandparents, aunts, uncles, cousins . . . we actually ended up visiting over one hundred relatives during our two-month stay.

So, this 1993 peace treaty was like the dawn of a new, brighter day. At long last, the international community had finally heard the calls of Rwandans who had been crying out for help, asking for assistance in returning to their homeland.

The other reason this is hard for me is because during this period I saw my dad's brother Kimenyi, and my mom's brother and sister Edouard and Goreth, for the last time.

They came to Burundi for a visit, and it was like Christmas! We were all happy, we danced almost every night, and our parents sat talking for hours, day and night. After more than 20 years of separation for my dad, they had a lot to talk about, they had missed each other!

Because there were still insecurities in Burundi, they came to us in Bujumbura, and I remember the walks we would take with my aunt Goreth, and the conviction I had that she was the most beautiful person I had ever seen.

I wanted to be like her when I grow up. She was pious, she was a member of the "abakobwa ba Musenyeri" "bishop's daughters", and she lived pure as a nun.

This will even be one of the many reasons Hutus of Kibuye hated her twice . . . first because she was a Tutsi obviously, and secondly because she had refused to wed any of them. They believed that she refused them because they were Hutus, whereas she was only keeping herself virgin for the Lord.

She was not a nun, but she lived as one.

Anyway, because of the ceasefire and the jobs that were being proposed to returnees in Rwanda, she was convinced that it was time for my dad and the whole family to move back to Rwanda.

Doctors were in big need, and he could have asked for any post anywhere in the country, she argued.

Together with my uncles, she pleaded their case so persuasively that dad was almost convinced.

So, in good faith, he told them that he first needed to find his replacement and sell his properties, and that in no time, he would move his family back to Kigali.

My aunt, testing his sincerity, requested that she and my uncles be allowed to bring mom and all the kids back to Rwanda, leaving dad in Burundi to wrap things up on his own before reuniting with us.

By some miracle, he declined, declaring that we would all go together later, when he would be ready.

But to ease her mind, he gave her permission to take two kids back to Rwanda, a gesture designed to demonstrate that we were all behind them.

She then took my brother Patrick and my sister Clark with her back to Rwanda.

When they got to Rwanda, Patrick stayed with her at my grandmother's house in Kibuye, and another Aunt Rose, who had just returned from Belgium to take up a job of Professor at the University of Butare, took Clark to live with her.

Back in Burundi, we all started preparing for our return to Rwanda.

In our minds, we were incredibly jealous of Patrick and Clark. We all wanted to go.

And since there were still instabilities in Burundi, this treaty had come at the right moment. This was like a blessing.

But what my aunt didn't know, what we didn't know, what nobody foretold was that in less than six months, they would all be victims of one of the worst genocides in the history of humanity.

She just couldn't have imagined that the peace treaty would fail. Nobody could.

So, as I said, this period is not a happy one for my family, or for any Rwandan.

My dad's affairs must have taken longer than planned, or perhaps God did not what us to be in Rwanda at that time.

The fact is, we were still in Burundi when the Genocide began, in April of 1994.

When we heard that the Rwandan president's plane, carrying both himself as well as the president of Burundi, had been shot down, fear struck.

As always, this was going to be used as an excuse for Hutu extremists to start killing Tutsis. It was always the Tutsi's fault, whatever happened!

Had the Tutsis not developed a fear of Hutu extremists out of the long years of torture and persecutions, and had there been even a small attempt from the UN peace keeping soldiers or the international community to try to analyze and interpret the situation long before, this genocide could have averted.

But the minute the plane crashed, Tutsis were filled with fear and they waited in their homes for what would happen.

Hutus who had been coached their whole lives, and prepared by extremists started blaming this crash on the only group that had been blamed time to time again—the Tutsis.

They were to blame, and they were to be killed; said the radio. Their first message on the national radio across the country became: KILL THEM ALL!

The propaganda over the years had taken root, and had borne fruit.

Even young children started chasing their playmates throwing stones on them, chopping them with machetes, and calling their fathers on them simply because they were Tutsi.

Some of these people, who had never studied or moved from their home villages, had no idea why they had to kill their friends, their partners, their children born from a Tutsi partners . . .

Except that "Tutsis were the enemy. Whatever happened was their fault, that they should let anyone escape, kill them all."

This was broadcasted on national radio starting from the moment the plane crashed.

They started calling Tutsis by name, declaring that they were cockroaches that needed to be exterminated; and that, just like cockroaches, they had to ***kill them all***, otherwise, even the small ones would mature and multiply.

So to make sure no one would survive to multiply, they would disembowel pregnant women and kill their fetuses, they would kill young babies by crushing their skulls against walls, they would castrate men before killing them in order to emphasize the denial of reproduction, they would humiliate women by raping them in front of their children and their husbands before killing their whole families in front of their eyes, and then either killing them or leaving them to rot or to be eaten by dogs, sometimes while they still clung to life.

They did it all.

The horrors that were committed in the 1994 Genocide were inhumane.

During previous killings, and I believe in the European war and revolutions it was the same; people had sometimes survived by hiding in churches, with priests oftentimes providing protection.

So, naturally, the first reflex of many Tutsis was to seek refuge in churches. Radio broadcasts declared that churches were exempt from being attacked, as well as stadiums, and public places such as schools.

Once again, everyone hoped that, as before, if only they could reach those places, they would be safe. They thought that, as before, only a few would be killed, and those who were in churches and other public places would be protected; that after one or two weeks everything would get back to normal, and they could then safely return home.

There was now an international force on the Rwandan territory; what harm could have come to them in their presence?

I remember that our aunt called to tell my dad that everybody had made it to the church, including my brother; they were all safe and sound.

Instead, she was quite worried for my sister since she was in Butare, a city of scholars, a city where the killings were particularly virulent, and organized by smart people.

Most Tutsi had managed to study abroad during their refugee time, and in 1993, many had come back and gotten jobs in all the sectors.

My Aunt Rose being herself a Bishop's daughter like my Aunt Goreth, was starting her life in Rwanda. So, to do so, she had taken two of her nieces among them Clark, and one of her nephews to live with her.

So, my Aunt Goreth worried as hell, and trying to get information as to how they were doing, left the rest of the family in the church and went in search of news from the Butare.

She needed to know if they were okay, for the sake of reassuring my parents. While doing so, she took refuge in a nunnery where lived European and Rwandan nuns called "Benebikira*". She worked there, and hoped to benefit from their protection as she waited for news.

Unfortunately, they soon realized that this time things were different.

The radio was calling on every Hutu available to put into action "The Final Solution," killing all Tutsis in order to wipe them from the face of the earth, or at least from the territory of Rwanda.

Neighbors started killing friends that they had hidden, groups of killers started forming and organizing manhunts, looking for Tutsis to kill, road block started to be created all over the country, and people were obliged to show their identities to show if they were Tutsi or Hutu, Tutsis being killed there at once . . .

Use your imagination.

Actually, I'm sure you won't be able to imagine everything that they did, because it was beyond comprehension.

Unspeakable things were done during this genocide that I simply couldn't begin to describe.

Sometimes, witnessing all the horrors, and fearing for their loved ones, people would beg to give money and other belongings to get bullets from the killers, and beg them to use them and kill them quickly.

A father would buy bullets for his whole family, to avoid torture and a "bad death", by offering his properties and all his belongings to the Hutu militia*.

Most of the times, they would accept only to laugh at them after and start enjoying torturing and killing them "URWAGASHINYAGURO" = "A SHAMEFUL DEATH".

If you ever listen to a survivor's testimony at least once, I'm certain you will never be the same again.

Now, by inviting people to join the public places, they had a plan: when all of the churches, schools, and stadiums were filled, only then did the Hutu militia reveal their true intentions.

Their plan was to get everyone where they wanted them, let them feel safe for a couple of hours, days, even weeks like it was in Kibuye, allow them to call or go fetch any of their relatives who had hidden elsewhere, and, once everyone was there, do what they had been planning for decades. *Execute the final solution* and: *kill them all!*

65

This is how almost all of my mother's family perished.

With the exception of my aunt, who was at the convent, they were all in the church . . . and no one survived.

After barricading the doors, they threw explosives into the church through the windows, one after the other.

And as if that wasn't enough, they would then come inside and finish, kill any who had managed to survive the explosives. In this particular church in Kibuye, very few survived.

And even these survivors were chased afterwards and killed, chopped with machetes.

This is the case for my brother Patrick and one of my cousins who had survived and ran from the church, but got killed later by a group of armed Interahamwe*. This was discovered during the GACACA* courts meetings in Kibuye, long after 2008.

One can count on his fingers the ones that made it to the end of the Genocide.

While the church was being attacked, a killing squad went to the nunnery and demanded that the nuns hand over any Tutsis they had hidden there.

Only my aunt Goreth was still there waiting for the news from Butare. They tried to hide her and, at first, refused to give her up.

When they refused, the killers gave them an ultimatum: either gave up the Tutsi they were hiding, or they would have to die with her!

It didn't take them long to realize that they were serious. My Aunt then told the nuns not to sacrifice themselves for her, and gave herself up.

Would they have done more to protect her? Probably yes. Would they have been safe doing it? Definitely *not*.

In a way, she kept them from being responsible of such a hard decision, because whichever decision they would have made, they would have regretted it for their whole life.

If they gave her up, they would have never forgiven themselves, and if not, they would have condemned themselves to death.

Well they didn't have to. Only one life was taken.

The Interahamwe squad took her to a public place where they tortured her to death. Some of the things people say happened to her are inhumane that I wish I could 'un-hear' them!

She was the most pious woman people had ever known in Kibuye. In addition of being a "Bishop's daughter*", she was beautiful, charismatic and lovable person.

Those who knew her called her a saint. Hutu men accused her of being proud and disrespectful of them because she didn't want to marry them . . . but they had forgotten that she wasn't married to any Tutsi either.

She had other priorities like praying, and being good to everybody.

But this did not protect her. She was tortured, multi-raped, took turns, and lynched in public as if she was nothing, nobody . . .

They did all this saying that they want to take away her pride, respect and belief that she kept so closed in her heart, and they failed.

People say that until her last breath, she kept her dignity.

But this made her murderers angrier, as they disgraced her and still felt disrespected. She remained untainted until they finished her.

And she remains as such in my heart, and the hearts of those who knew her! She was kindness and beauty personified! She will always be my role model!

As for my dad's family, they had been killed during the first few days following the plane crash, because they lived in a village.

In the small towns and villages, neighbors who knew the people who were supposed to die, never waited.

The minute the radio started chanting *"Everybody, start working . . . you know who's the enemy . . . exterminate them,"* they started working!

So we never heard of any survivors, and we have no idea how, when, or where they were killed.

What we do know is that a family made up of more than 30 people disappeared from the face of the earth, as if they never existed!

My uncles and Aunt had kids, and my grand-parents were still alive. They all got killed within the same days.

I will always remember my twin uncles, Kimenyi and Kimonyo who looked alike so much that they used to play us pretending to be the other back in 1988. My Aunt Tamari, the last born and the only girl in my dad's family shall be missed as well. In that summer we were there, she got married and had already 2 kids by 1994.

Together with all the other family members, they all perished!

At my aunt Rosie's house in Butare, where my sister Clark was staying, things quickly got complicated as well. The day after the crash, a killing squad came directly to the house early in the morning.

Fortunately for my aunt, she had left the day before to visit her sick friend in Gisenyi, and had ended up spending the night. It was in a nunnery.

As soon as killings started, they hid her in the ceiling of the house for days, before they could get them to safety and be able to flee to Belgium, a place where my aunt had lived and studied before.

Meanwhile at her house, the only people at home were the three children.

When the militia entered, Clark hid herself behind the curtains, and from there witnessed the massacre of her cousins.

They were about to leave when one of them said that there was supposed to be a third child. So they started looking for her.

When they were on the verge of finding her, she came out, grabbed one of the killer's hands and begged him for her life, saying things a nine-year-old could say: "*Please forgive me, I will never do it again* . . . not knowing really what she had done or why she was begging for mercy . . . ! *You are my dad, you are my mom, I love you, I will do anything you want, I beg of you, Please don't kill me!*"

Something she said touched this man, because he then vouched for her and said that he would take her to his home, to his wife, and that, if needed, when he will feel like it, he would kill her himself.

His fellow killers thought about it, and then let him take her home.

She stayed with him for a week. Every morning the guy would go out to "work"—to kill more Tutsis—and would come home in the evening covered with blood, but never fulfilling his promise to kill Clark.

And then one day, as if by some miracle, he sees a Red Cross truck pass by his house.

These were some humanitarian organizations, based in Bujumbura that would go to and from Rwanda, mostly transporting injured people, or medicine; sometimes picking up orphaned kids wandering in the streets.

So, this guy—God bless his soul—saw this as an opportunity to save my sister. Clark had told him that her parents lived in Burundi, so he gave Clark to them, and told them to help her search for her parents. They promised and took her with them.

Obviously all Rwandan families in Burundi were in shock, overwhelmed with the news they were getting and especially on the images on Televisions showing what was happening.

Nevertheless, it didn't stop them from wanting to help as much as they could.

So, every time a truck would arrive from Rwanda, parents would come to pick up kids to foster and orphans to adopt.

Clark remembered the name of our Aunt Espe who live in Bujumbura, and had given it.

Luckily, a friend of hers coming to pick up kids to foster was asked if she knew her, and she did.

They immediately contacted her, and still not believing in what they had just told her on the phone, went to pick her up.

Remember, in our minds, Butare was more dangerous than Kibuye in the beginning. So we were sure that Clark, together with our cousins, was dead, and we held only slim hope for those who were in Kibuye, in the church.

We had no idea that Clark had survived.

We were reunited by coincidence, or should I say by miracle?

Our Aunt Espe immediately contacted my dad, who took a car and went alone to see her, and confirm if she was serious, because he just couldn't believe his sister. He had to see Clark himself to be sure!

Clark is our family's miracle.

Of all the family members across Rwanda, those who were in the Rwandan territory, she and one other cousin Bedette were the only ones to survive.

And she survived thanks to that killer with a slight kind heart.

We have never found out who he was or why he did it. We only know that he gave us back our sister.

We pray that wherever he is, he finds favor that is equal to the one he rendered to us.

CHAPTER 9

When I relive all these experience, it's like a nightmare. Right after the genocide, it was hard to believe.

Sometimes I would wish that it was all a dream. That I was asleep, and wish that perhaps when I would wake up, my brother and my aunt would come walking through the door.

Unfortunately, it was all true.

You must be wondering how I could possibly know the details of our people's deaths, or for about the details of the Genocide in general.

Well, you may have heard of the justice system in Rwanda called *GACACA*, which was part of a system of community justice inspired by tradition and established in 2001.

The aim of this system was to promote truth, justice, and reconciliation among the people.

In these sessions, a group of *Inyangamugayo*, well-respected elders of a district, elected by the people, would sit down and preside over the proceedings.

These proceedings were mostly conducted in a manner of storytelling. People would say from DAY

1 of the genocide, where they were, what they saw, and what they did.

If one would try to conceal some facts, by lying or failing to mention all that he or she witnessed, others would confound him or her.

Most of what happened came to light. People would describe what actually happened, in real-time. Even in places where everyone had died, one of the perpetrators or his relative would tell what he or she had witnessed.

Many perpetrators cooperated, in order to benefit from the reduction of sentences that came with their confessions, others did not.

But those who did helped retrace the whereabouts of many, especially in identifying the improvised tombs where people had been buried.

Many people had no idea whether their relatives had been killed, if they had been buried, or, if they had managed to survive, where they had ended up.

This was because, often when Tutsis were running off to hide, they would get separated from one another along the way, some never being able to meet again.

So, through these *Gacaca* sessions, many people managed to discover where their loved ones were, dead or alive . . . but mostly dead.

Bodies were recovered from everywhere. There were many that were already buried all over the place; some were thrown in used toilet holes, sometimes while they were still alive; others in the river Nyabarongo . . . .

Some were found in destroyed houses under the ruins, or simply in holes dug by the perpetrators themselves.

This was not out of compassion for the dead; they were just trying to hide the bodies from the eyes of journalists and internationals that were still going around in the country.

So, immediately after the Genocide it was imperative to track down as many bodies as people could, and try to bury them with honor, what they had been denied.

It was important to start burying the ones in the streets as well, especially for the sake of the living.

There were broadcasts on national radio as well as on television—when it started working again—communicating about places and times of burials of Genocide victims in every district of the country.

For a long time, even until now, when remains of the Genocide Victims are found, they are given a respectful burial. It is all that we could and can do to say good bye.

People had grim tasks when remains were found: first, to gather the cadavers from wherever they could find them; then, to try and identify those they could by examining their clothes or in some cases, if they were lucky, by checking documents found in their pockets.

They would then give them a respectable burial, with prayers and a proper benediction.

Most of the time, all the religious leaders of the district in question would be present, to unite in their prayers for a peaceful rest, hoping that God would hear them better!

I used to go to and hear these prayers, these masses . . . but when it came to actually visiting the graves especially when they are still open, I wouldn't dare.

To date, I have never visited a memorial center in Rwanda! I haven't been able to summon up the courage.

I was always afraid. I'm still convinced that if I had to do it again, I would do the same.

Subconsciously, I feared the day I would come face to face with my brother's dead body, or that of my Aunt, or someone I knew.

Although I had seen many cadavers, I hadn't seen a close family member's dead body until my father's death on January 25th, 1998. This is why in addition of losing my dad on this day, this was and will always be, the worst day of my entire life.

I've already passed by commemoration centers many times. In fact, before one enters the Catholic Church of Kibuye, where my mom's family perished, and where we go for Sunday mass when we are in Kibuye, there is a memorial for the victims who died there.

But whenever I go to church, I do my best to look away when I pass by them. I am afraid of what I would see if I looked into the orbits of the skulls lined up there.

I've seen pictures; I think that it is enough.

I always want to remember my brother as a person, with passion and great love, my Aunt Goreth as a tall, beautiful woman, and my grand-parents, Aunts, Uncles, and cousins as I remember them in 1988.

Healthy, full of life, loving and ALIVE!

CHAPTER 10

Anyhow, while people, and not human remains because this diminishes them, were being found and being given a dignified burial, as much as it could be given back to the beloved deceased, the country was coming together.

I was angry almost all the time. Everybody was angry . . . frustrated . . . sometimes not even knowing why, or at whom to direct their rage.

And when you would know towards whom direct your rage, you would be bound by the law to refrain yourself.

Normally growing up, I used to, and still am trying to, strive and be gentle, generous, and kind. I'm a people person. I always have a smile on my face, trying to make everybody around me happy.

I believe that instead of dwelling on to the negative, I'd rather smile, keep my optimism and hope for the best!

But slowly by slowly, I began seeing that the world was going to be a tough place for me to live in.

I started wondering why this had happened, if life was worth living, and, if so, if I should be nice to people, knowing that tomorrow I could be their victim? Or why not vice versa?

I was afraid of what a man is capable of!!! I started imagining our future in Rwanda. I could not see a happy ending.

The tunnel was as dark as the hearts of many Rwandans at the time, and there was no light at the horizon.

For instance, when schools started reopening in 1995, we obviously went back to our classes. All parents wanted their children to stay in line and not to fall behind in their studies.

My siblings and I went back to school immediately. My older sister and I were still waiting on the 6th grade results from our Burundi primary school, but just couldn't wait longer; so we enrolled in the first year of secondary school.

Somehow we never went back to get our results; we just continued on from there, quite successfully I might add.

Schools had been destroyed, with school materials having been either stolen or lost.

We started in the halls of some industrial complex, in Kigali. Most of the time, classrooms didn't have windows or doors anymore, with some of the spaces half bombarded. But it did not stop us, and it did not stop the government from encouraging people to lend a hand in the rebuilding process.

For the first time since the Genocide, we were faced with the concept of living together with everyone— Hutu, Tutsi, and Twa.

Personally, with the education I got from home, from my Christian parents, I didn't mind being with the other kids, whoever they were.

But this didn't keep me from feeling the tension between the students, especially the grownup ones.

I even remember back in the 3rd year of my secondary school, somewhere in the south of the country, I witnessed a physical altercation between Hutu and Tutsi students, during commemoration period.

You must understand that this was, still is, and always will be, a sensitive time for all Rwandans.

Especially, it is super-sensitive for the survivors and the orphans.

At that time, some Hutu kids had insulted, or trivialized the commemoration day; and somehow they ended up getting beaten. I wouldn't say that I condoned this, but I did not condemn it, either.

I was very afraid that something worse would happen, but fortunately it ended with the arrival of the police, and no one was seriously injured.

Francine Umutesi

The commemoration period is a sensitive time; even if someone doesn't have anyone to remember or anyone to mourn, they should just keep quiet and let others mourn. Let us mourn!

It is quite impossible to imagine someone who doesn't have anybody to remember or to mourn though . . . Everybody lost someone at some point.

I am sure you are wondering about the relationship between Tutsis and Hutus from after the Genocide.

Imagine a place where Jews would be kept, together with the Nazis, some of them being the very ones that tortured and killed their families.

And in this place, they would tell them to respect each other, to live with one another, to study together, and most importantly, to forgive each other.

The world would be offended, and the Jews would feel betrayed, right?

But probably because there was the whole world and their own country for the Jews to go to . . . and probably because the Nazis had as well their own country to go back to and hide, and had the whole world against them, things went differently.

In Rwanda, RPF all by themselves had just stopped Hutus from killing Tutsis, but unfortunately had had to witness the horrors that Hutus had just committed under the surveillance of the UN, the International community, the whole world's watch.

They had a lot to deal with, a whole population to account for, and a country to stabilize. It wasn't easy, because everyone was on the verge of going crazy.

There was on one part, few survivors, injured and traumatized, who had no idea if they would ever feel whole again.

On a second part, there were Rwandans who were returning from their country of refuge where they had stayed for too many years and didn't want to stay there no more. They had hoped to find their loved ones, or at least some survivors. But some of them, like my mom and my dad, found deserted lands and destroyed houses. And cadavers all over the place!

There was a third part of Rwandans who were family members of the Hutu perpetrators, who had cooperated willingly or passively to the massacres, but had not fled the country. They didn't know what to do, and although some of them were waiting mostly for the revenge to come thinking that the Tutsis would make them pay for what their people had done, others were still feeling bad for not finishing the job, and exterminating the "enemy".

There was a fourth part, some few Rwandans Hutus, who had refused to participate in the massacres, who had helped and hid few Tutsis here and there, who had their family members massacred as well because they had refused to kill Tutsis. They didn't know how they should behave, they knew and had witnessed what their fellow extremists Hutus had done, and they had nothing to add.

And last but not least, there was Rwandans soldiers of the RPF, who had lived the horrors on a daily basis. Wherever they would liberate and take control, they would only find a trail of bodies, blood, tortured women and children, all that you can imagine. They had the first chair to the show, and it wasn't pretty.

So, when I say that there was trauma, I mean it. The whole population was traumatized, some more than the others, many in an irreversible way.

But despite the tensions following the Genocide, sometimes in public places, sometimes even in the neighborhoods, the Rwandan Government at the time and FPR Inkotanyi, now a political party, led the people towards a better understanding of their needs.

They did this by involving everyone in the Unity and Reconciliation process, and including by identifying the needs of everyone as a whole and fulfilling them.

Oftentimes they were criticized by all Rwandans, we all felt misheard, or even mistreated at some point. Obviously, to be able to control such a crowd with divergent ideologies, some wishing to get revenge for their loved ones, others having no remorse but thinking of ways to finish what they had started, and others not knowing on which side they are on . . .

But the government accomplished the impossible, they got results. They got everyone to chill down, and to think of the most important thing for all: respect for life.

Anyone who knows the Rwanda of 20 years ago, then 10 years ago, and then today, will tell you how far the country has come.

This progress wasn't accomplished in one day. And it wasn't easy.

There were many struggles, too many struggles.

The population was confused, unable to trust again. Then, when everyone understood that there was only one Rwanda, for all Rwandans, and that there was no other way but living together, life took its course and went on.

CHAPTER 11

Well, I myself can tell you that I have very good friends from both groups, and we don't talk about our ethic origins at all.

For a long time, Rwandans had lived with the names Hutu, Tutsi, Twa in their conversations too much. Before the Genocide, people identified themselves not as Rwandans, Africans or human beings, but as Hutus, Tutsis and Twas.

It was time that this changed.

It's true that right after the Genocide it was hard to imagine a peaceful life with everyone.

But with the guidance and the presence of the RPF, the Rwandan government led by the first President Bizimungu, then by our current President Paul KAGAME, Rwandans managed to set aside their differences, to try and see farther . . .

They decided to work together so that they could build a country for their offspring.

Because, although some of the Rwandans were supported by foreigners such as French, they realized that there were no consequences for them. Only Rwandans were hurt, and only the perpetrators that were punished were Rwandans.

They understood that when they were destroying Rwanda, they were only setting themselves back, and nobody else.

Well, some of them did understand this.

Anyhow, I remember that people started to avoid certain topics of conversation that would raise ethnic controversies, depending on whom you were talking to.

But now, subjects that divide us rarely come up in conversation, and even when they do, the awkwardness has diminished. We discuss things that are of importance.

Many of us know what's in our best interests. Not killing each other, but striving for a peaceful and prosperous country.

I say many of us because there are still some bullheaded people who will never let go. But many Rwandans just want *peace!*

Our focus has now shifted to things far more important than petty differences in personalities and family trees. People, mostly the young, are now more interested in science and technology, in how to build our country together, for everyone's benefit.

Nowadays, people believe this: If Rwandans keep killing each other—Hutus killing Tutsis, and eventually Tutsis taking revenge—and vice versa . . . —after a few years, a few decades, the country would end up being deserted.

And this is certainly not what any Rwandan really wants!

This is not what I want for my kids, or for our future generations. This is why we all had to listen to the voice of reason, and forgive, or might I say tolerate each other for the sake of peace.

In general, school was fun for me. Of course, after all the horrors, people were not the same.

But I can say that I had a normal high school experience in a boarding school in the south of Rwanda, with my classmates from both Hutus and Tutsis, and my brothers and sisters did as well.

It wasn't without stress, but it was exciting and instructive, just like any high school in any part of the world.

Meanwhile, people were being encouraged to participate in the reconstruction of their country, not only by rebuilding the infrastructure and homes that were needed, but by rebuilding the most important pillar of every society: PATRIOTISM, TRUST in the community.

It was one thing to convince some 10-to 18-year-olds to live together, tolerate one another, and study together, but it was quite another to persuade grownups, who had seen what their neighbors were capable of, who had lost trust in each other, that they should live together and trust each other again.

Meetings were organized as often as possible. I can cite: *Umuganda* (mandatory Community Service Day) was initiated and still takes place, as a mean to unite everybody for the purpose of getting them involved in the development of their district by working together, their security by discussing any disturbance at the end of umuganda.

Then *Gacaca* sessions, that were organized at least two times a month in every district of the country.

Anything that would bring people together to discuss the current affairs of their districts was attempted, in order to preach unity and reconciliation to people.

This was done for all age groups. I remember that there was this program in which young people who had taken their high school exam in order to get to University were also required to attend what we called *Ingando*—a place where Rwandans are taught all there is to know about their country.

I did my *Ingando* in the summer of 2000. It was extremely instructive!

During these Ingando, authorities from the lowest to the highest levels would visit us, discuss with us and answer any questions we would have, presenting lectures on topics of concern in Rwanda, especially our controversial history.

But the main course there was about Unity and Reconciliation! The history of our country was explained in detail, as our people—our ancestors—really experienced it.

We were shown the price Rwandans and Rwanda as a country had had to pay to get where we were by 2000—the losses, the blames, the insults—but also the successes.

Facts were presented to us. We came to understand what the divisions and hatred had actually done to our society, a society that had lived peacefully for hundreds of years before. We were taught why Unity and Reconciliation were our only options, our only hopes for building a peaceful and prosperous country for future generations.

We had the opportunity to meet the Army Commander at that time, who explained to us many things about Rwandan tactics against all the attacks that were being directed at our country.

We came to understand why Rwanda had really entered Democratic Republic of Congo, and the status of the whole situation by 2000.

None other than his Excellency President Kagame came as well at our *Ingando*, and like he does it every time he meets with the people, he talked with us. I really mean that he talked with us, and not to us.

I should emphasize that President Paul Kagame, is the man who led the way as Rwandans fought and still fight for the freedom of their country, and still are.

Like Patricia Crisafulli, the co-author of the best seller book "RWANDA, Inc"[3] said: "President Kagame operates more like a company CEO than a political leader. He is totally focused on the attainment of goals, building strong institutions, security, discipline and good governance, more like what a real corporate leader would do".

So like he had been doing and still does with the whole population, he was ready for an open discussion with us.

And again, for the first time in my life, I envisioned myself as a politician. The one who doesn't lie, but sits down with his constituencies and tells them the truth!

I understood that, at long last, this was a country that was worth living for, worth saving, and worth giving a chance—not by the international community, not by the UN, not by anyone else . . . but by *us!*

---

[3]   http://us.macmillan.com/rwandainc/PatriciaCrisafulli

I understood that we needed to give ourselves
a chance to a peaceful and prosperous country.
Because nobody would give it to us!

I still remember everything in his speech!!!

There were always things that one would hear on
foreign radios or TVs, and get confused, but here
we got to ask questions to the man himself.

I got all the information that I needed to feel safe
again.

Since this *Ingando*, I felt peace for the first time in
my "post-Genocide" life. I knew that I had someone,
a government, and a whole army in fact, who had
my back, and who had the interests of all Rwandans
at heart.

From that time on, I stopped worrying about what
was going to happen to us, or whether or not the
Genocide perpetrators living in Congo would ever
come back to kill us. I stopped worrying at all.

For many generations, history has shown that
Rwandans, and indeed most Africans, I'm sorry to
say, have been living in fear, waiting on the West,
and simply following orders.

They had never actually given themselves a chance
to try and build their own country. They were and
most of them still are always waiting.

When I express this sentiment, it is because this is how I felt. There was always that ongoing feeling of waiting: Waiting to see when the UN would decide to get involved and help the stateless Tutsis, when they would come to decide whether this was a Genocide or not, waiting to see when the UN would decide whether or not they would help the widows and orphans of the Genocide, waiting to see how much they would be willing to give . . .

We wondered if there would be sufficient funds to open enough schools, enough hospitals; wondered when the international community would remember the poor people in Rwanda, victims of the total destruction of the country and the economic crisis in the region.

There was always a certain spirit of waiting, in me, and in many other Rwandans.

After the *Ingando*, I understood that I was on my own, and Rwanda was on its own. The only things that mattered to me now was struggling to survive, spreading Unity and Reconciliation to those around me, at the very least living in peace with my neighbors, whoever they were, and striving for the development of my country to the best of my ability.

There was not going to be much help from anywhere, and the sooner I understood that, the sooner I would start helping myself, my family, and from there my own country.

This was mostly a wake-up call for all young people fresh out of high school and ready to go on to University to continue their studies.

I'm sure this was helpful for many, giving them the motivation that was needed to understand their own needs, and those of our country. I know it changed my way of seeing things, my way of seeing *life!*

CHAPTER 12

Back at home, in the villages, towns and the cities, people were communicating as well, mostly through *Gacaca* court sessions.

For instance, It was during one of these sessions that we uncovered the story of how my brother Patrick really died, along with one of my cousins.

It turns out that they had not died with the others in the church, as we initially thought, but managed to survive the explosives only to be killed later. Here is the story of how it happened.

One afternoon, sometime in May 2000, during a *Gacaca* session, a prisoner told the story of two kids that he had killed with his squad, in his neighborhood.

My mom was present at the session, and, at first, had no idea who the guy was talking about. He told about two kids who had survived the church's bombardment.

Remember when genocidaires threw grenades into the Kibuye church? Somehow, there were a few survivors. The prisoner explained that they would go in with machetes to finish them off.

But, there were a lucky few who would hide under cadavers, covering themselves with blood, hoping to be invisible to the killers. Amazingly, 2 kids had survived and later escaped.

They ran back to their neighborhood, and were hidden by one of my mom's Hutu neighbors. They began hiding in the maize plantations during the day, coming out at night to eat and to get some sleep.

Then one evening, a guy that had come by to visit happened to see them.

This guy, instead of keeping it a secret, immediately summoned a killing squad. The Hutu woman had hidden them for almost two weeks.

So when the killing squad heard this, they immediately went after my brother and cousin, searching until they found them and cut them with machetes!

In some situations, they killed both the Tutsis and anyone would have helped them. This time, however, the woman had given them away quickly enough to save both her life and the lives of her own family.

I certainly don't blame her. I think that she helped them as much as she could. The only thing I blame her for is that, even though she came to work for my mom in 1995 and had been working for her ever since, she had never mentioned anything about it.

Not even once. We thought that all our relatives had perished in the church, period! She may have had many reasons for keeping quiet: perhaps she was afraid of what we would think of her, or that we would blame her somehow.

But still, learning of it in a public place, and from someone other than her, was shocking, and definitely disappointing. It was certainly crushing for my mom.

The person who had called the killing squad was also present at the session. He had never gone to prison for murder or massacres, and no one had accused him of anything before. So he didn't think that anyone would say anything now.

But, would you like to know who he really was? He was one of my mom's colleagues, and had been working with my mom for about three years before this story came out.

He had had many opportunities to tell my mom, but had never said a word.

He was one of their drivers, and he would drive Mom to and from work almost every day. He would even volunteer to drive her even when she was off-duty.

He was "nice to her" in a way that made him seem unusually thoughtful.

My mom did not mind, considering that in the city of Kibuye there were no taxis, no buses, and we didn't have a car of our own. So she accepted it, assuming that he was just being nice.

At that *Gacaca* session, everything became clear to her. He had had remorse for getting my brother and cousin killed, by calling the killing squad on them, but had never found the courage or the guts to tell the truth; not to my mom, not to the authorities.

When he was outed, he ran to my mom and begged for her forgiveness. And you know what? Despite the tears in her eyes, despite feeling her wounds reopened and her heart once again shredded into pieces, *she forgave him!*

Right there! And this was total and chistian forgiveness—not a cover-up, not some sort of tolerance move—*sincere* forgiveness!

She told him that "if he had repented enough, if he had regretted his act sincerely and was ready to make amends as asked by the *Gacaca* court, and if he had asked God for forgiveness and gotten it, who was she to refuse him?"

As punishment for this and other same kinds of acts he was found guilty of, he was sentenced to community service time for a number of years, and now lives happily with his family in Kibuye.

When Mom came home and told us about it, we felt so powerless. I wanted him to be punished more; I wanted to scream . . . but I did nothing.

Instead, I admired my mom's strength, and spirit. I don't know if I would have reacted in the same way. I definitely would have had some reservations about forgiving the guy right away.

But this was actually the second time I knew of in which Mom had responded both mercifully and serenely in the face of an extremely tough situation.

There was a previous time when I witnessed just how much kindness and forgiveness my mom has in her heart.

It was the first time when she visited her hometown after the Genocide, only to find that her entire family had been decimated, their houses destroyed, with anything that was left having been taken by neighbors who still lived there.

One could have even assumed that they had been our relatives' killers—but not my mom. She went to their houses, and, even while recognizing some of her mother's clothing, household decorations, and other things, exclaimed that she was happy to see at least someone from the past, someone who hadn't either fled or died.

She did not claim those things; instead she let them keep them, except for photos, which she took back.

Some of them are still in our photo albums, half-destroyed after having been out in the rain for a long time before being taken by those neighbors.

Unfortunately, others were completely unsalvageable, and had to be thrown away.

We were glad to have recovered some of these pictures, because It helped us meet some of our relatives that we hadn't met back in 1988, or babies that had been born after our visit.

In addition, these neighbors had been exploiting our mother's family land since our family had left.

So, what did my mom do then? She told them to continue their exploitation, but with the condition that they would at least keep some of the bean and maize harvest, as well as some avocados and bananas for us. And she would even give them the grains to plant.

Anyhow, many had gone to prison or even died for less. But, as my mom would always say, why would she be angry at them when all they wanted was to survive and to take care of the things nobody was there to take care of?

As long as they were not the ones who had killed her family, she had no feelings of reproach towards them.

Therefore, she was going to be normal, kind, and generous to them, as her family had been long before her. And she was, and still is!

Whatever revenge we sought in our hearts, however painful we felt, Mom would always say that nothing would bring our loved ones back to life. That instead of looking for people to blame, we should just have pity on the killers.

She would say that they were in more pain than we were; that being responsible for such slaughter was punishment enough.

She would say that God would decide whether or not they would get away with it, God would decide whether or not He would forgive them.

She, as a mere mortal, was not the one to judge them. She told us that wherever they went, or however they escaped, justice would be served, but not by her hand, or her heart.

Then, after all this, she would add that she would neither blame nor condemn anyone for what they had done, for they were not themselves.

They had temporarily become savages. Meanwhile, she says that she will simply wait, and the only thing she will do, will be to ask God a single question, when she meets Him face to face: *"Why?"*! Why did He have to allow this, to leave her alone, and to let Rwandans sob this much??? WHY?

She is a devout Catholic, and she even is nicknamed *"Madame Jésus"*—"Mrs. Jesus"—by her fellow churchgoers in recognition of her devotion.

I guess Jesus is going to be in trouble when they finally meet!

CHAPTER 13

When we decided to move from Kigali, Kibuye
wouldn't have been our first city of choice.

As you can imagine, there were too many memories
there for our mom. There were also too many
people, many Hutus and almost no Tutsi survivors.
It was just too painful for her, and for us, to resettle
there.

But, after our dad's passing in 1998, my mom had
had too many responsibilities to manage, and all of
us to bring up alone in Kigali city.

We were still in high school, my younger brothers
and sisters in primary school, it was just big a
burden to bear for her, with no support from a
brother, a sister, or a parent of hers.

In addition, although she had a small business
before, she was jobless at the time because she
had been robed. So, Dad was the only one who
carried the weight for bringing money home.

She tried to find a job as a teacher, and managed
to find it in a nursery school at a private school for
toddlers for a year. Eventually, she decided that the
salary wasn't enough to keep us living in the city.

It felt right to go and live in Kibuye, because there at
least, our mom was owner of her family's land which

was not small considering that it had more than 5 families living on it, my uncles and aunt's families. More than 100ha, and there was nobody to claim it or even live in it any more.

She wouldn't have to pay rent like she was paying in Kigali. It would be one expense less, seeing as she was paying our school fees and our up-bringing, all by herself.

Fortunately, she soon found a job as a social worker with the Ministry of Local Government (MINALOC) shortly after we had settled in Kibuye, starting in 1999 and lasting until 2004.

She works since with a French Association that takes care of Genocide Orphans known as "Orphelins Rescapés du Rwanda" "Orphans Survivors of Rwanda".

In brief, we had chosen to move to Kibuye because it was her birthplace, hoping for a better life and easy one for our mom.

There was no one else who could have helped us otherwise—not financially, not even morally.

We had lost all our parents' relatives in the Genocide, all our cousins; only remaining with our Aunt Espe's family, who, like us, lived in Burundi, and of course my uncle Kiza's family as our only relatives.

And as you may imagine, they had their own struggles for survival, they couldn't have helped us in any way.

Furthermore, the government was struggling to deal with the Genocide consequences of all kinds: trying to support women who had been raped and had contracted AIDS, as well as many other diseases; orphans who had survived with no other relatives to look after them; a country whose population was almost erased from the face of the earth, and a Genocide that was being denied, etc . . .

Having nowhere to turn, people had to find ways to solve their own problems, with no support from the government.

We were grateful to have a country, and to feel secure. The rest was just an everyday struggle that we all had to deal with.

But after our dad's passing, life just seemed too hard, almost ubearable!

We were more than fine before, in the post-Genocide period; our dad was a doctor, and earned enough money for the household.

And in addition to his salary, enough but not that much, my parents received food rations from the hospital staff, mostly given by Humanitarian NGOs who were supporting the government.

So, compared to the average Rwandan, we were more than okay.

But the minute Dad passed away, with no other source of income, there was no way we were going to survive in Kigali without all these privileges.

Since we were all still in school, we needed school fees, and we of course needed to be fed.

In addition, houses in Kigali were tough to afford for people without good-paying jobs.

Although my mom had avoided it as long as she could, the only solution was to move to a place where we would not be obliged to pay rent, where we had a chance to survive.

Normally, for a doctor who had worked for many years in Burundi, and who had worked as much as he could, sometimes day and night, after the Genocide in Rwanda, one would think that the Social Security Fund could have done something to support his family.

Well, they could have, if not for our bad luck!

First, when we left Burundi, we were in such a hurry to get back home, to flee from the obvious threat we faced, that my dad left all of our properties unsold. So, after a while, he had to return to sell them.

He went back, sold them for the very little money they were offering; because Burundians knew that Rwandans would accept anything just to be able to part with their belongings, especially the un-movable ones.

So he brought back all the money from the property sales in a suitcase—mostly because back in 1996, no banks had reopened yet; the banking system was very slowly starting to work.

Someone who knew what he had done in Burundi, who had followed him and knew exactly that he had sold his belongings and had the money at home, came with armed accomplices, faces covered, to our home during the night and stole all of it!

They took everything, even the loose change that was on the nightstand.

The only thing that my dad had bought from this money on his way back was a minibus that he had put in Kigali, which was working as a mini-bus taxi.

So, the next morning we had hope; we were not going to die of hunger. The daily money that the taxi brought home could sustain us until his next salary . . .

Unfortunately, just two months later, the same bus was in a terrible accident, which killed seven.

It was never fully repaired, and the insurance coverage was used to pay the families of the victims.

We never got anything from it. My dad actually told me that he was even going to go to prison, because a bus malfunction had caused the accident, but the charges were dropped.

So, we were lucky at least that he remained free.

All these events, in addition to the trauma of losing his whole family in 1994 caused him so much stress that in 1997, for the first time in many years, he had his first diabetic crisis.

My dad had lived with diabetes for 29 years, since he was very young, and in my entire life I had rarely seen him sick, let alone critically ill.

But this time, it was serious. He was treated and, fortunately, it was during the New Year's holidays, so we were all at home from the boarding schools and could help care for him.

I remember that we returned to school on January 4th, 1998. I was feeling relieved; he was better; all was good.

But after that incident, I was worried. I had seen my dad sick and helpless for the first time. I feared for him, and for our entire family. He was everything to us.

So when on January 25th, one of Dad's best friends Cyprien and an aunt Berna, came to my boarding school, and went directly to the headmistress's office, I immediately felt sick. Literally. I saw them, and I felt dizzy.

10 minutes later they came out, and school officials told me that I was to leave with them at once, that I was needed at home.

This was the first time this uncle or even this aunt had come to my school.

Note that in our tradition, we call all our father's or mother's close friends uncle and aunt when necessary, as a sign of respect.

So, for them to come and pick me up from school, it was serious. I immediately knew that something was wrong. I asked them what was going on, and they would only tell me that I was needed at home, that it wasn't a big deal. But that I had to hurry.

On our way back, they told me that we had to pass by my sister Ally's school, to pick her up as well. And again, my heart skipped a beat in my chest.

I was now certain that something had happened, but I didn't want to think about the worst; I couldn't accept it, and I couldn't let my imagination wonderer off thinking about it. I just refused to accept what was becoming clear to me.

Just after picking up Ally, they pulled the car over, and talked to us saying: "Hey girls, it's about your dad. He . . . ," began our uncle.

I then let out such a scream . . .

I didn't let them finish, I was devastated. I screamed "noooooo" and couldn't stop crying . . . We both couldn't!!!

It was as if my heart had just been ripped from my chest. We cried all the way home, a trip that took about an hour.

When we arrived, and I saw all those people present at the vigil, I couldn't refrain myself, I screamed again and couldn't stop crying.

Our dad had died on the morning of January 25th.

To date, I wonder what my life would have been if he was still here, what all our lives would be like.

Too much have happened, I am now a mother of two beautiful girls that will never know him . . . The pain is still fresh, but experience taught me that life goes on!!!

We had to continue living, despite everything . . .

So, as I was saying, as if this suffering was not enough, when Dad died, in early 1998, the Rwandan Social Security Fund was still three months away from finalizing the documentations necessary to register employees and start planning for their retirement at his workplace.

He died before he could sign anything. As a result, he was never registered, and although he had worked for more than 30 years in the health care environment both in Burundi, and later in Rwanda; his family did not benefit from any kind of support.

People had been massacred by their neighbors; others were still dying because they didn't have access to hospitals.

Our dad, who had saved many lives of others and had done many other selfless good deeds, had just died, and the world was not coming to an end.

The world was continuing to go on.

He had had diabetes for 29 years; he had injected himself with insulin every morning for as long as I could remember, since I was born, and he had treated himself with care.

The proof of that care is the fact that, in an African country—Burundi, then Rwanda—with no advanced medical technologies, he had managed to survive for 29 years, only to die when we needed him the most.

He was the head of the family, father not only to his kids, but also to his sister Espe's kids, our cousins who had lost their dad towards the end of 1994.

We all looked up to him for everything.

His death shocked us, touched each one of us, in such a way we have never recovered from!!!

Thereby, misfortunes were coming at us one right after the other. But because of all the horrors I had witnessed, I was numb to the pain, until my dad's death.

I knew we would overcome everything and that he would always be there for us. But life is just that. With it always comes death. In the face of death, I now know how powerless even the most powerful people must feel! There is nothing one can do, when death strikes . . . Now I know.

Anyhow, this is why, in order for my mom to find a way to support her large family, she decided that we needed to go and live on her family's land in order to save on rent money.

Her family home had been destroyed by the genocidaires, as had all other Tutsi houses and properties, because they said that if they couldn't have the Tutsis' properties, nobody could, especially not the RPF Inkotanyi, who was winning the war.

The genocidaires' propaganda was that they would not let them inherit an intact country, so they took their time, especially in the west of the country, and destroyed everything in their path.

I should mention here, that the reason they took their time in the west of Rwanda is because there was what the French called a peace mission, "Operation Turquoise"*.

This was an operation carried out by French militaries, with a mandate from the UN pretending to come to the rescue of the victims who were getting killed in Rwanda . . .

It was a cover-up, because they only came to protect the "government of Rwanda" during the Genocide, helping them to terminate the remaining "job" of exterminating Tutsis, and to help them flee to DRC (Zaire at the time) and abroad. So they occupied the whole Western country comprised of a part of Gisenyi, Kibuye Gokongoro, and Cyangugu . . . which make all the exit routes from Rwanda to the DRC.

These gonocidaires did not limit their given time to destroying properties only; they took their time to gather, look for all the survivors who had managed to hide from them until then, and exterminated them systematically under the helping, approving and protective eye of the French military!

"Operation Turquoise" was approved by the UN Security Council, but in reality they did not know what was their real mission, nor that the French officials had a completely a different agenda!

Like my mom, many Kibuye born people don't have even one survivor to tell the story . . . they were ALL pursued and chased, and finally massacred!

So, when we got to Kibuye, she had to rebuild her sister's house of four rooms, so that we could move and live there.

For a Rwandan family in Kibuye, this 4 room house was more than enough. It had a sitting room and three bedrooms, with a toilet cabinet outside.

Cooking is mostly done out in the open air on charcoals, but even during the rainy season, we managed to go on with our lives. At least we had a roof over our head.

Anyway, it was hard on our mom, because the last time she had lived there, she'd had her whole family with her; those that we had met in 1988.

So imagine returning there, only to find the land decimated, with no houses and no living relatives, and living there ourselves. No wonder she took refuge in Christ, and prayed daily and night, there on deserving her nickname "Madame Jesus".

We had no other option.

If we did, we would have gone to live somewhere else, *anywhere* else but Kibuye!

My sister and I were away at boarding school most of the time; we were home only during holidays.

I was always worrying. You see, most our neighbors had at least one family member in prison, meaning that they had participated in the Genocide. And we had no way of knowing exactly who had killed our loved ones and who hadn't at the time.

I used to fear that someday we would return home only to find our family dead, something that happened in many other places.

But, as I said, we had no other options. At least we had no rent to pay in Kibuye, and mother could worry less.

In addition, we had a land where my mom cultivated beans, bananas, maize—that way she could do something to feed us, and she could even sell some produce to pay for our school fees.

Some of the people who helped her work the land were questionable and untrustworthy.

But again, there was no other way of knowing who had done wrong and who had not. And she couldn't have handled the work alone.

Whenever we would tell her of our fears and suspicions, she would always say that God was watching over us, that He was our protector and that nothing would happen to her, or to us.

Nothing did happen to us. But In all these years, we did learn a lot about our fellow human beings.

CHAPTER 14

Since we had returned from Burundi to Rwanda, it had been too hard for my parents to go back to their home villages.

I remember that during our first three years back in Rwanda, they took us there only for few visits, and only bringing me and my older sister Ally.

I remember once going with my mom, on her first trip back. We visited my mom's place, as well as my dad's. It was so unreal. I remembered running all over the place with my cousins back in 1988, going down to Lake Kivu, swimming most afternoons. Now, there was nobody left!

There was nothing, only lands that had been tended by neighbors, houses in ruins, destroyed during the Genocide, and people watching us as if we were aliens.

Those who remained in the country were either families of the genocidaires who had stayed behind and refused to flee with their murderous relatives; families of Hutus who had refused to participate in the Genocide and had managed to stay alive themselves; a few Tutsi survivors who had just come home from wherever they had hidden, sometimes from the swamps; and us, who had lived abroad for many years.

And because we refused to stay abroad for a minute longer, we were astonished to see all the horrors that had happened in reality. TVs had not shown everything. Not at all!

After the Genocide, when we were coming *home,* to a place where we had longed to come, we only found cadavers all over the place: in the streets, in the ruins of houses, in toilet holes—*everywhere.*

I remember that we entered the country from Burundi, passing through the southeastern region Rwanda, a region called Bugesera, home to millions of Tutsis that had just been exterminated.

They say that the government of Habyarimana had sent them there because that area was infested with the infamous "tsetse fly." The government's hope was that the flies would kill off the Tutsis and they could avoid getting their own hands dirty.

They used to say that in spite of all the killing, Tutsis still somehow managed to survive. And though many did die from the tsetse, others still lived there, surviving in spite of everything.

The spectacle that was awaiting us on our way wasn't pretty.

On our way from Burundi to Kigali, passing by Gashora and Nyamata, we witnessed unimaginable scenes.

There were human cadavers, some torn by dogs, others already dry. There was nobody to bury them, so they were still lying exactly where their killers had left them.

In houses, you could see whole families still stacked on top of each other, piled like pieces of wood, their blood already dry. In some situations, rain had spread pools of blood all over, especially on the streets, and we had to see all that.

I was only 13, and my youngest sibling was just three. But what we saw opened our eyes in so many ways. It was beyond our imagination, beyond anybody's imagination.

It was the first time I had seen a dead body, and I saw tons of them.

When we reached Kigali, the streets had been cleaned a little, just for the sake of allowing cars and people to pass. But if you went through an underpass, or took a small shortcut, you were sure to find piles of cadavers taken from all over the neighborhoods.

And the smell . . . it was unbearable! I couldn't imagine that what I was seeing had been human, or that they had been turned into those smelly things by other human beings.

I didn't want to think about people I knew in this way. I refused to believe that my brother, my uncles, aunts, and cousins were also like that now—just a pile of "things" that smelled, that we all wanted to get rid of.

I felt bad wishing those cadavers to be gone, wiped off the streets, out of our sight, because I wanted them to be alive, to be with us at the same time. Each time I would see a cadaver of a boy, a girl, a woman, or a man, I would immediately imagine seeing one of our dead relatives.

And because the Genocide left many orphans and people alone on the streets without homes, every time I would see someone passing by me, I hoped I would recognize one of our cousins, or my brother.

So, I invented myself a fantasy, a dream that I kept hidden inside of me, for when it would become real: I hoped that maybe one of our cousins, or my brother, had survived and was just lost. I would convince myself that somehow he was given away by the Red Cross to some people who had taken him abroad, and that someday we would find him/them someday.

And of course, it stayed a fantasy, it never came real! Because we now know that no one will ever come home. They all perished.

When we arrived in Kigali, many other Rwandans were also returning from exile.

The RPF Inkotanyi had stopped the Genocide, but unfortunately they were not able to avoid hundreds and thousands of losses.

Hutu extremists had killed every Tutsi that they had met, chasing them all over the place. In many places, they had planned the right times to kill them by lying to them and calling them to come hide into public places, into churches . . . promising to let them live.

They had even managed to plan their own escape, with the help of their French allies; When they were about to lose everything, the French government put in place the infamous "Opération Turquoise," in which western Rwanda came under their control.

The RPF Inkotanyi was not allowed to go there for almost 2 months, under the surveillance of the international community. This was along the border with Zaire, which is now the Democratic Republic of the Congo.

Like I said before, this operation covered Kibuye my Dad and Mom's home place, as well as Gisenyi, Gikongoro and Cyangugu. This is probably the reason why we never had any survivors in our whole family! They cleaned the place up!

Obviously the French did this in order to provide protection and time for the genocidaires to flee, and they even helped in the search for Tutsi survivors to finish off.

In Bisesero, they observed while genocidaires fought with Tutsis who had taken to a school for refuge, and who struggled to survive for days, until they were eventually overcome, massacred with the help and in front of the French soldiers!

I remember that we weren't able to go to Kibuye safely until the following year, 1995, because this place was still feared, and we didn't know who or what we would find there.

Now, after the Genocide, many people were thrown in jail. Like I said, no one knew who had done it, or if the neighbor back in your hometown was a killer or just an innocent bystander.

So after the genocide, mostly in Gacaca sittings, people started to talk, survivors started testifying against their attackers, and some killers started confessing, denouncing their peers who wanted to hide from justice.

Others began hunting those who had survived, mostly to prevent them from testifying against them.

Chaos reigned once again.

People say that the FPR Inkotanyi committed murders as well during and after the Genocide?

Well, we were back in Rwanda by August of 1994, and what I remember is that right after the Genocide, Tutsi people wanted revenge.

They were so angry, so driven; they wanted to practice the philosophy of "an eye for eye". Some of them would have been legitimately deserved, because sometimes a Hutu wife and her kids would stay behind, while the husband who had killed all their families would be away, or in prison.

Obviously, this provoked a lot of animosity, a lot of resentments and hate. People wanted their own form of justice.

But nothing like that happened.

Instead, the RPF and the government put in place institutions that would protect all Rwandans, whoever they were; and of course those who disobeyed the law were punished exemplary.

They called for Rwandans to live together.

The message was clear: "Rwanda was and always should be for *all Rwandans."*

Whether we liked it or not, we were supposed to live together. The country was neither for Hutus nor for Tutsis *alone*. It was for *every* Rwandan.

Even the genocidaires had the right to a fair trial; hence the punishments against those who sought justice for themselves.

I remember having murderous thoughts as well. I was a 13-year-old with no grandparents from either my mom's or my dad's side, no more than four cousins, and no other family in the whole world.

I saw how our country had been treated by the international community over the years, and I was angry.

But then we were taught that what happened had happened, and that being angry and murdering others wouldn't solve anything!

That would only make us murderers as well; it would make us inhuman, beasts . . . no better than those we were seeking to punish. The circle would go on and on, and then what?

Our only option was to strive for a better Rwanda, a peaceful Rwanda, and a prosperous one.

A Rwanda where our children's children would live in peace, where Hutus and Tutsis wouldn't see each other as enemies, but as the neighbors they always were.

But most of all, a place where people would stop seeing each other as Hutus and Tutsis, instead would start thinking of themselves as Rwandans.

To tell you the truth, I was skeptical. The whole world was skeptical!

I didn't believe that I myself, let alone survivors, would reach that stage, where we would feel fine living with everyone as if we were all the same.

Neither did the International community. Some people still question the truth of this sentiment over Rwandans . . .

But it became a reality.

Our current government over the years has been criticized, our president categorized as a dictator and a murderer.

Those who voice their opinions should know first our history, and the context in which one becomes a dictator if any, or as I like to fondly tell people when they insist on calling him a dictator, President Kagame is and will always be the father of our new nation. And if he is a dictator, I want to be like him. Getting peace and prosperity to a devastated land, getting Rwandans to live together again in a calm environment . . . who wouldn't praise such a man?

As far as murder is concerned, I have no idea who president Kagame murdered, or when, or where he did it. As a soldier, he definitely was the best since he single handedly managed an almost fallen army, and brought it to victory, thereby ending the genocide against Tutsi alone!

With his high standards and sense of humanity, I doubt that he has ever done anything that wasn't necessary, first to defend himself, and then to defend his family, that is ALL Rwandans, and for the prosperity of his people, of ALL Rwandans.

But calling him a dictator—with my definition of it when it comes to him as a "father of a nation" and a "necessary dictator",—I actually support and admire him for this.

Understand that I am not accusing him of being one. But if people want to keep this word in their vocabulary, I believe that they should add some adjectives in front . . . to me, and to many Rwandans, he is a *heroic* dictator, a father that would do anything to see his children safe and prosperous!

Because no "dictator" as the international community understands it, would have the interest of his queens at heart, he wouldn't fight for the freedom of his people, and then share the power with everyone, bad or good, just on the promise for a better nation.

No, as Rwandans see him, or as I see him, *he is a kind, heroic and necessary dictator.*

Living abroad made me come up with this analogy mostly because when people asks me where I am from, and I would say Rwanda, they immediately would ask me what I think about Kagame, and ask if I agree that he is a dictator or not.

So, instead of starting arguments as to why he is not a dictator, I would start telling them why he would seem to be called such a name in the first place.

The understanding of dictatorship for Westerners is fixed, whereas in our country, it has lost its meaning when people were on the verge to act as animals. When there was such chaos, that only a firm hand could manage.

If it weren't for him and his fellow FRP Inkotanyi soldiers (the Rwandan Patriotic Army RPA), that became later the Rwandan Defense Forces (RDF), there would be no country to call Rwanda, nor peace and prosperity for Rwandans.

I will try to explain.

When the Genocide ended, soldiers went back to their hometowns and, as you can imagine, discovered that their families and friends had been massacred. In your opinion, what would be your first reaction, if it were you?

They obviously had their weapons. few of them, one of whom I know personally, took matters into their own hands and tried to avenge the deaths of their families by killing family members of the people who had murdered their loved ones.

But the minute one of these soldiers was caught, he was punished with the death penalty.

It was so serious that some soldiers and survivors got angry at the head of the government, wondering why they would go so far as to protect families of the genocidaires. At that time, it made no sense to a lot of people.

But nothing kept the law from establishing order, peace, and security for all. People were being punished exemplary, so that the rest wouldn't dare make the same mistakes.

Folks started behaving themselves, some out of fear of being executed, or being thrown in jail, others by understanding the real challenges that were ahead for all of us.

People began coming back from abroad, and the interim government helped by the RDF soldiers started trying their best to make the country habitable.

They started reorganizing the country: getting hospitals up and running, as well as schools; trying to provide clean water to the population, since water had been contaminated by the cadavers that were everywhere; trying to get people to live together and respect one another; trying to get businesses open and get the people what they needed for everyday living.

Drastic measures had to be taken. No one was really willing to do his part. Most of the Rwandan people were just too traumatized to deal with whatsoever, let alone improving their country.

Over the years, long before the Genocide, the media had been used to convince Hutus of the evil inherent in Tutsis, of their duty to cleanse their homeland of those enemies, those cockroaches.

Well, this had to change.

A decision had to be made; laws forbidding this to happen again had to be passed.

And the media became an instrument for reconstruction, diffusing messages of Unity and reconciliation all the time!

For instance, some of these laws had to ban all media in Rwanda from preaching anything promoting Hutu, Tutsi, or Twa ethnicity, or rekindling the genocide ideology.

Broaching the subject is punishable by law, with no exceptions. Is this a dictatorship? Is this bounding the press from free speech? I would say NO, with capital letters.

This is saving a country, this is saving a people!

In order to save and protect the Rwandan population, many decisions like these had to be made. And not everyone was ready to be blamed, to be responsible. President Kagame was.

People may call him what they want, he will always be our hero, my hero. Without him, there wouldn't be any place worth calling home to any Rwandan!

There wouldn't be any place that I call home!

CHAPTER 15

Houses in Kigali after the Genocide, as well as lands in the whole country were tricky to get ownership.

First, because there was many people who were returning back to Rwanda, and who owned nothing there like us. These were the many people who had lived abroad for more than 30 years, who had come back to their home, to find the void.

Secondly, because some of the owners had been massacred, sometimes entirely, others fled from their home places going either to Congo, or abroad or just in other provinces in order to avoid their neighbors recognizing them and testifying against them.

People had fled the capital Kigali, everything was in ruins, shops had been looted, and there was chaos everywhere.

People like us, who had just packed few of their possessions and come back to Rwanda, had nowhere to sleep, nowhere to go. So it made sense that people would enter any empty house and repair it, in order to make it livable, and stay in it.

Some people were "lucky", if I may call it luck, to find houses in which no one had survived, or a house that belonged to killers who had left the

---

country, and managed to live in them for a long time. Some are even still living in them.

But my family and I lived in three successive houses: each time the owners would return, and we would be obliged to move on.

Just before our dad died, he had acquired a piece of land where he had started to build our own house.

To top it all on our misfortunes, the person from whom he had bought the land was not the original owner, but the "post-Genocide" owner.

The deed was eventually taken from us, and this person was never found. With our dad gone, there was no chance we could have ever managed to find him, let alone prosecute him. So we let it go, and decided to go and live in Kibuye!

Now Kigali is a beautiful city that is still hard to live in, but only as hard as it can be to live in any fast growing city.

Yes, the country has come from really really far!!!

20 years after the genocide, the destroyed houses have been rebuilt, better yet, skyscrapers are all over the place, housing projects have been executed, and the city is recognized among the cleanest cities in Africa, if not in the world!!!!

If there is one thing Rwandans should be proud of, it should be their courage, their tenacity, and their strength.

What Rwandans lived in 1994, and long before, should have caused a nation to disappear. Instead, it made us stronger!

When one hears the motivation quotes and all that, one thinks that it's all just "crap".

But I and many people who have followed the history, the disasters that Rwandans encountered, the losses that we all suffered, and the way the country is striving for a better tomorrow, I am amazed.

CHAPTER 16: FORGIVENESS

Whenever I hear that word, I always wonder what it really means for the person saying it.

At church, they teach us to forgive others as we would like them to forgive us. Well, it was, and still is, hard for Rwandans, but not impossible!

Most other Genocides were generally committed by people from one country coming to exterminate people from another country.

And when it's all done and finished, everyone would return home, where they would live with the consequences of their "post-genocide" being individual.

Whether these consequences are hurtful, bad, or worse, they lived them among themselves, and had the time to heal, before they can be faced with the topic of forgiveness, if ever.

In that kind of environment, forgiving can seem possible, even acceptable, because they are never obliged to see each other again, unless by choice.

The particularity of the Genocide against the Tutsis made forgiveness even harder to imagine.

It was the same people, from the same country, from the same *village*, from the same *family*, who massacred their own. It was a long life of torture and exclusion.

Parents killed their own kids because they were from a Tutsi partner; neighbors killed their friends of many generations, even some of whom we call "blood brothers"—two families bound together by traditional customs "kunywana" and some blood ceremonies that used to be performed in ancient Rwanda turned on each other.

So, it is a genocide that is and will always be difficult to forget, let alone to forgive.

But, surprisingly enough, people were able to forgive, or at least to *tolerate* each other.

I say *tolerate*, because it was easier than forgiving entirely. It was more attainable.

The road to forgiveness, however, was a long one.

Responsibilities had to be taken and victims taken care of. Most importantly, there can't be any forgiveness if nobody is asking for it.

Well, despite that other parties had participated and supported the perpetrators, and that others had just watched, Rwandans had only themselves to rely on.

If I neglected to emphasize it previously, this is the truth: the Genocide was stopped by *Rwandans alone*.

In a modern world, where systems of communications and means for intervention are what they are, Rwandans stood alone.

Following World War II and the holocaust, the United Nations adopted a resolution in December 1948, stating that "the contracting parties confirm that, genocide whether committed in time of peace or in time of War, is a crime under international law which they undertake to prevent and to punish".

So if the massacres in Rwanda were in fact Genocide, why did the world turn a blind eye?

After many years of exile, then an attack that was supposed to open the international community's eyes and get them involved; after a peace treaty that was being ignored by some of the political figures In the Rwanda of 1993-1994, and in the world, no one believed that there was going to be a genocide, let alone that they had the obligation and the duty to save those in need.

With the exception of blaming them for attacking the "legitimate government" of Rwanda, everyone ignored the FRP Inkotanyi.

Yet, with no special powers or any other support, the FPR Inkotanyi somehow managed to stop the Genocide. They were not as well-equipped as the "legitimate government," which had French support; they were not better trained.

What they did have were a strong will and a driving motivation, factors that are more important than anything else!

Yeah, they had the *"will,"* something that people never seem to consider as important, and the *"motivation"* to go and save what they loved most: their families and their country.

As the Genocide began, even though there were journalists and peacekeepers from all over the world in the country to follow both the peace treaty signing and the UNAMIR; very few saw, or anticipated, what was being prepared and later carried out.

And those few who did see it and tried to prevent it and later to show the horrors that were being committed were shut down as quickly as possible.

Even when videos and images managed to get released, some still didn't believe, or didn't want to.

So, the only hope remaining was the Rwandans counting on themselves. The FRP Inkotanyi couldn't just patiently sit back and wait for international help while their people and their country were being destroyed.

They struggled to keep the remaining ones safe, to save as many as they could.

This was the first time in the history of Rwanda— at least since the colonial period—that a group consisting of both Hutus and Tutsis, without segregation—were fighting for the same aim: liberating their country not only from Hutu extremists, but also from the control and manipulations of some Western countries.

And this was the first time that *all* Rwandans understood that they had something to lose all together: their country.

As I said before, though it was clear that the primary goal of the Genocide perpetrators was to wipe all Tutsis off the face of the earth, they also began to destroy infrastructure, everything they could, so that no one else would profit from the country, should they be defeated.

In the years leading up to the Genocide, some Hutus within Rwanda had realized that the country was going to ruin, instead of prospering.

They had seen that separating politics were not going to help anybody, but keep the country backwards.

Therefore, not only did Tutsis chased from their country want to return home, but there was also a clear need of change among many people within Rwanda itself.

I think that some Rwandans had begun to realize long before how Tolerance, Acceptance, and

Forgiveness were going to be their only allies in the coming change of their country.

So, after the Genocide, as I mentioned before, no one wanted to accept responsibility for the victims, or for Rwanda as a country.

They didn't even want to refer to what had just happened as *Genocide*; everyone was afraid of the possible repercussions.

The international community was astonished by what was being said, what was being shown, what was being discovered about the whole massacre; they did not wish to be blamed.

Not the French government, who directly aided the perpetrators and was afraid of being associated with them; definitely not the UN itself, which had soldiers in place and had them abandon innocents they had protected for some time in Kigali, leaving them to a certain death.

When I think about it, I always wonder how the world works, how it is really run.

If this is the process for all peace missions, missions whose budgets would be enough to buy food for millions of hungry people in the whole of Africa, or South America, or Asia, and more; if this is how the UN deals with their many crises in countries around the globe, I was amazed that we don't have many more genocides and catastrophes. *Seriously!*

"If a powerful country says one thing, nothing happens, but if that same country says something else, things start to happen!" And so it goes . . .

As I mentioned, this is a story of many lifetimes.

All this started long before I was born, before my parents were born.

For a long time, problems in Africa have always had something to do with the need to be understood by Western countries; to be accepted—approved—by them.

So, during the period of over four decades in which Rwandans were being exiled, being killed, I haven't found evidence of anyone who tried to help out—at least not successfully.

At first it was considered the Belgians' responsibility to solve the problems as they saw fit; later, the onus was on the French. And these people did nothing more than exploit the situation.

It is the story of every African country and their colonizers, each in their own way. But I will not go there. I will only insist on the fact that, because of this, many lives were lost, people were unjustly treated, and countries were mistreated.

When the UN was being created, it is my belief that there were situations that led to its creation. There were crises in Western countries, and most of the international laws and decrees that were created were developed to prevent and protect the people against such specific events, in specific situations.

But as the world became bigger, and third world countries started getting involved, these laws would prove to be inadequate.

They have never been adapted to the situations in these countries. Most times, misunderstandings result from the differences in political, economic, social, and environmental situations.

For instance, the way we deal with everyday problems in Rwanda is not the same way that people do in the US, in Asia or in Europe.

I can understand why an American or a European would call a person like President Kagame a dictator, since he insists that whoever fights for the benefits of only one group of people, Tutsis, Twas or Hutus shall be punished by law. What they don't bother to understand is why this actually, *is* a punishable act in Rwanda.

History, ever the good teacher, helps us to avoid repeating the same mistakes. Instead, acting differently and responsibly should be encouraged.

Traumatized people who have lived through the horrors of Genocide would normally require a long period of healing, lots of "cancelling sessions". It took Rwandans mere days and months, however, before they were able to let go, to tolerate, and, to forgive for the blessed ones.

It's not such a big surprise; Rwandans have always been a forgiving people. If you look at our history, even the recently developed *Gacaca* legal justice system, traditionally people have been drawn towards forgiveness and making amends, rather than punishment.

Later, when the other kind of legal justice came, this spirit of forgiving did not end. Although there was much violence, people were becoming Christians, and learning about Christian forgiveness. Among themselves, they were good to one another.

After the Genocide, considering the massacres committed in Catholic churches all over the country, people began questioning their faith, their religion.

In addition, back in 1993, Pope John Paul II had visited Rwanda. This made Tutsis wonder, whether he knew about the plan to kill all Tutsis, considering his support to the government of the time, and question his role in all this.

This was most questionable, especially when the Vatican began using a waiver of immunity for priests who were involved in the Genocide, protecting them from the courts of justice, and giving them asylum in Rome.

I would like to mention here the impeccable behavior of Muslims during the Genocide, in most Rwandan cities. There is a "quartier" called Nyamirambo in Kigali that was home to many Muslims before the Genocide, and still is today.

These Muslims are comprised of both Hutus and Tutsis.

During the Genocide, the Hutus hid the Tutsis in mosques, keeping them safe until the soldiers of FPR Inkotanyi came to their rescue. They even stood in the way of some Interahamwe, who wanted to enter and massacre them.

All Rwandans agree that these Muslims were wartime heroes. Heroes because this was the only religion, or church, where a group of Hutus actually stood up for their friends and managed to save them. Of course some isolated cases of Catholic churches and others exist. But many of them did allow the horrors to be committed in their place of prayer, except for these Muslims!!!

So, in light of all this, people were spiritually confused after the Genocide. Some converted immediately to Islam; others turned to the Protestant and Evangelical churches that opened their doors immediately following the bloodshed.

There were churches springing up everywhere, even in prisons. Ministers began preaching forgiveness, and telling people that the End of

Days had come, the time when "fathers would kill their own children and children would kill their own parents." So, it was imperative for people to save their souls, to put an end to murderous and vengeful thoughts.

These calls got heard, all right. People converted, others repented. They had nothing to lose, and nowhere to go. They had lost faith in the Catholic Church, and in the world.

Anyhow, my theory is that Forgiveness was possible not only because the Unity and Reconciliation Commission was powerful enough to convince people to unite, not because, as some people say, there was a dictatorship in Rwanda, but also because people were feeling "godly".

After such a horror, people were stunned, and could hear their souls either cry with anger, vengeful thoughts and sufferings, or with reproaches for what they had just done.

Of course there were, and still are those ones, who are not convinced, and still want things for this or that group only.

In any case, I know for a fact that this ameliorated the relationships among many people, and it surely made lots of prisoners repent, and compelled them to speak the truth about what they had done.

But most of all, it was made possible by a government who's aim was to insure everybody's security in the whole country, to ensure that everyone have an equal chance to life.

CHAPTER 17

Writing this book is a way for me to deal with my losses, as well as my gains. It's not because I am a Rwandan that I admire what has been done since.

But it is because I am Rwandan that I am writing this book.

President Kagame once said that "If we don't tell our story, somebody else will tell it, wrongly!"

And you wouldn't blame that person, right?

I started reading books at the age of 6. I still read a lot, anything that I can get my hands on: romantic novels, scientific books, historical books, magazines . . . I just read everything.

You would be surprised by the amount of information one can get just from reading.

So, this got me thinking. What if Rwandans, myself included, were just misunderstood, because people didn't know anything about us, anything about what happened to us, or anything about what really happened—and continues to happen—in our region?

Wherever I travel, mostly in Europe, people ask me if I am a Nigerian, or an American because of the color of my skin. When I answer that I am a

Rwandan, they give me a "weird look" before asking me if I'm Tutsi or Hutu.

All Rwandans have found themselves in such a situation at least once. Fortunately, I am no longer ashamed, as I was in Burundi before the Genocide, or even right after the genocide, to say that "NDI UMUNYARWANDA": "I am Rwandan", and proud of it.

Explaining who you are, and why you can't divulge your ethnic group, but only your nationality because it is what matters, has become every Rwandan's duty, wherever we go.

Living and studying in Europe has made me realize that, although we learn geography, history, and other people-related subjects in school, we will never truly know other people's personal experiences—their ways of living, of surviving, their everyday struggles and victories—unless we read books specifically about them, personal experiences being the best narrative and the most detailed way.

Some of my friends don't know much about me, and definitely nothing about my family. They might know my name, my mom's name, and my kids' names, but they don't really know *me.*

I was talking about cancelling earlier. Sometimes I wish that I had someone I could talk to, someone who would carry my burden with me along the way, who would tell me what to do whenever I feel like screaming . . .

Francine Umutesi

I hope that writing some of history will give me some peace, and will let people know that underneath this smiling face, underneath *every* smiling Rwandan face, there is pain, loss, hopes, history, and faith.

Whether fiction or non-fiction, I love to read books and watch movies because then I can imagine the chapters that might follow the ending. In this case, it is an ongoing story.

My family's journey continued, and still continues. We've had many tragedies, and lots of happy moments since the loss of our dad to Diabetes in 1998, and the moving to Kibuye. We've endured it all with dignity and self-control, sometimes with despair but still managed to survive it all, because of our love for each other.

Since all this, since 2000; we have all grown up.

And just like in every lifetime, you find the same events: I am now a single mother of two beautiful girls, and although I hold a biomedical engineering obtained after lots of struggles and sacrifices, still doing a second degree and working in Europe, it is still an everyday challenge to earn enough and to support my mom who provides for my kids and my younger siblings.

I hope the future holds better circumstances for us, but as it is still unknown, one can only hope that it is full of a bright future and realization of our biggest dreams.

148

My older sister Ally is married with two daughters and a baby son; Wera is married as well with 2kids, Clark already finished her Law and Administration degree and is currently looking for a job, and my younger brothers are both currently finishing their Bsc studies one in Finance, the other in Accounting.

The struggle has been so long, and so hard; but because of the bond that unites us, the love we share, we always come through!

We always have each other's backs, and always will. It is the only thing that can help us found new families, and make up for the lost ones. It is the only way that we will honor our dad, and our loved ones lost in 1994.

Our love will help us to build a new family tree that will not end with just a couple of branches, but will spread towards the future with as many as possible.

And our love for our country, my love for Rwanda gives me a reason to wake up, and think of a way to do better so that my kids and their kids can inherit a country without animosities . . . not anymore.

I can't but highlight that there are still big scars even though some of them are not visible to the naked eye; people still feel like it was yesterday, but they know that they have to look forward, to the future.

The past will never be forgotten for sure, but people want to try and live for a better future.

But then again, I have to emphasize that some traumas will live with us forever.

There are many who were crippled during the Genocide, lots of women who were widowed or contracted diseases from being raped, orphans who had to raise themselves, and many other consequences on one hand.

On the other hand, there are others with invisible scars.

For instance, the fact that up until this moment I have never entered a memorial place, or a Genocide grave, is disturbing.

Even after all the bodies I saw lying on the streets, after everything I've lived, and all that I've seen on TV, I still haven't had the courage to go and view the skeletons and skulls that are on display. I still want to keep the memory of my brother and my relatives as they were, not as skulls.

I don't want to go there and start trying to imagine who is who, perhaps even try to recognize them from their skulls, and if I can't, to start imagining and remembering them as such.

I refuse to think of them as just bones lying there!

Perhaps I will eventually pay them a visit with my two daughters, to whom I owe an explanation.

They are still young to understand, but at some point, and even though I'm delaying this until they are older, they will need to know, they will need an explanation soon.

I will have to explain to them all that happened, and why they don't have as many relatives as the other kids at school. But for now, I have to figure out a way to deal with it myself.

Just like any Rwandan, if you introduced me to the person who really killed one of my relatives, the one who killed Patrick with his or her hands, even though 20 years have passed, I am pretty sure that I would be very upset, and perhaps wouldn't forgive them immediately.

But I would live with them in the same city, in the same village, even in the same house. Do you know why?

Because I would want to do better; I would want to respect their lives, to show that I could be better than they are. I would want my kids to live in peace with their kids, nobody chasing anybody, and I would want to eventually die with hope for our future generations.

This is just a tiny little example of how much Rwandans were touched by this Genocide.

And I am sure that there are even far worse traumas.

Mine, I shall keep and cherish them, because no matter what I say, no matter how serene I feel forgiving and moving on, I shall mourn my brother, my Aunts, my Uncles and my grand-parents for the rest of my life!

But also, I shall remember the pain I felt, the despair I saw in my dad's eyes, the tears I saw on my mom's cheeks, and know that I as well as anybody on this earth have no right to inflict the same to somebody else.

As much as I can, I shall strive for peace, and for the freedom of all Rwandans.

There is no place for divisions in Rwanda anymore. If people haven't understood the price to pay, I have. And many other Rwandans have too.

And long as we still have President Kagame with us, as long as we still have Rwandans who are willing to sacrifice themselves for the prosperity of our country, we shall overcome every animosity.

Calling him a "dictator" or treating him as some people treat him; will not erase what he did for us. He gave us back a country to call home, he gave us a reason to live, he gave us a purpose, and he gave us peace.

He is the one who taught Rwandans to behave, to "love" one another again, and this is what I will surely teach my kids.

Most heroes are recognized after their death, he is an exception to the rule!

Forgiveness, as hard as it can be, was possible not because Rwandans are more capable than any other nation or more forgiving, but only because what we experienced occurred under unique circumstances; it took unique actions to overcome it, that only WE can appreciate the depth, and the need to forgive and live again.

CHAPTER 18

Current situation in Rwanda can attest of this.

Over the years, and after so much, Rwandans have now understood that there is more to life than preoccupying oneself with differentiating rather than uniting and peaceful ideologies.

There is a notion of unity, patriotism and focus towards our country more than ever.

This was made possible progressively, and thanks to the effort of President Kagame, his government, and of course, it couldn't have been possible without the cooperation and the will of all Rwandans.

Every year since the Genocide, starting from 1996, Rwandans have always remembered the Genocide trying not to get back to it, but to learn from it.

And every year on the 7th of April, we remember.

And every year a "theme of the year" is announced by the Organization IBUKA, which translates as: REMEMBER.

Here is the list of these themes as we remembered since the end of the genocide:

In 1995, wounds were still fresh, and people were still having resentments, they were angry . . .

People were still thinking that somehow justice should be done, whether it's by killing those genocidaires, and taking revenge, whether it was by blaming the world for not helping out . . .

There were lots of ideas as how to honor the fallen that were still all over the place, some not even buried yet. There was still the sentiment of powerlessness, people wondering if they could have done more to prevent it.

The title chosen was related to this entire situation:

1995: *"We did not anticipate it, we did not see it"*

Then as the years passed, depending on the situation the country was found itself in, and also depending on the people's need for motivation, themes continue to change every year, for the best.

Every Rwandan now live for these themes, because every year, we can identify ourselves with what the country is going through, and feel our responsibility,

In addition, every year an assessment is conducted in all the levels of the government, to try and evaluate themselves in order to discover how much the country have managed to fight in achieving the previous theme's mission, and what should be done going forward.

Listing them here will show how far we have come, and which direction Rwandans are choosing to take.

1996: *"Let's fight against bad governance, reinforcing Justice by promoting the culture of peace and reconciliation".*

1997: *"Let's fight against genocide, by bringing back our beautiful Rwandan culture"*

1998: *"Let's remember the Genocide, 4 years later!"*

1999: *"We demand that Genocide perpetrators be brought to justice, and be stopped from erasing the evidences that incriminates them!"*

2000: *"We denounce who ever wish to make us forget, and to deny the Genocide!"*

2001: *"Let's remember the Genocide, while building our country!"*

2002: *"Let's remember, fighting against Genocide ideologies and deeds!"*

2003: *"Let's remember the Genocide, supporting all the efforts for Unity and Reconciliation!"*

2004: *"Let's remember and eradicate Genocide by a collaborating with the whole world!"*

2005: *"Let's remember, by fighting the Genocide ideology in Rwanda, and in the world!"*

2006: *"Let's remember the Genocide, by participating into GACACA courts and having* the courage to tell the truth and by facing its consequences!"

2007: *"Let's remember the Genocide, by lending a hand to the survivors, and striving for justice!"*

2008: *"Let's remember the Genocide for the 14th time, by fighting to eradicate its ideologies, support the survivors, and promote the development!"*

2009: *"Let's remember the Genocide against Tutsis, fighting against its denial, and building our country!"*

2010: *"Let's remember the Genocide against Tutsis, improving the effort in the fight against the traumatism!"*

2011: *"Let's remember the Genocide against Tutsis: Supporting the truth, promoting self-dignity!"*

2012: *"Let's remember the Genocide against Tutsis, learning from the past, to shape a brighter future!"*

And last year's theme was special.

2013: *"Let's remember the Genocide against Tutsi, as we strive for Self-Reliance".*

This theme came at a time when Rwandans once again, had to stand alone, and fight for themselves.

A time, when the only logic of the situation at hand was so confusing and so difficult to overcome, a situation when our lives made only sense after striving for Self-Reliance.

This theme talks about relying on oneself!

To detail a little about the context of this theme, let's go back in history for a bit.

When the 1994 Genocide against Tutsi was being premeditated and later being perpetrated, nobody wanted to pay attention. Rwandans dealt with it and stoped the killings by themselves.

Then, started the period when the *genocidaires* who had fled to DR Congo (formerly, Zaire) started what is known in KinyaRwanda as *udutero shuma* "small attacks" in the north of the country, decimating a large number of people most of whom were survivors of the Genocide.

The International Community was too busy trying to ignore what had just happened that they did nothing to prevent it, or let alone help Rwanda protect its population. What happened then?

Rwandans again took the initiative of going into DR Congo, not to trample on the sovereignty of an independent country, but to prevent more attacks by those "genocidaires" to the western part of the country.

Regarding this, everybody had a preconceived judgment, mostly blaming Rwanda for entering Congo.

But like I said, because NOBODY did anything, Rwandans had to protect their people by themselves again!

The international community unrelentingly blamed Rwandans for all the instabilities that followed in Congo, forgetting to understand why they had engaged in Congo in the first place; ignoring the fact that they had left as soon as the country recuperated and agreed to cooperate in the stopping of the "Interahamwe" murders; ignoring the fact that Congo had their own issues to solve as well; forgetting that except for the wish to stop the continuing killings of the Congolese people of Tutsi origin in the Eastern DR Congo, Rwanda had and still has no other interests in that country.

Many other facts were displayed as well . . .

The conflicts kept occurring, and the blame on Rwanda continued.

And to top it all, a group of UN experts led by Steve Hege, published a report accusing Rwanda of "funding and participating actively into the DRC conflicts, by supporting the M23 group and much other nonsense" in 2012.

Now, I am not going to discuss the veracity or the wrongness of these allegations here. I will only argue that once again, the UN failed Rwanda! Plain and simple!

I will discuss the reaction to such allegations from the world though.

First, without checking the proofs brought by these experts, without asking Rwanda for explanations, without even conducting a thorough investigation that would have clarified the situation for everyone, the UN and the International Community reacted immediately by withholding the financial support they had agreed to give to Rwanda.

Just like that!

And like always, they expected Rwanda to bow down, confess their misdeeds, even if there were none, and beg for the release of the help.

Instead of trying to talk to Rwandans, try to understand . . . Rwanda was ONLY to blame.

In all this, at no time, did anybody try to come in aid of Rwanda . . . they all assumed that it was all true.

As before, Rwandans told the truth about what really was going on in DR Congo, but nobody listened . . .

Well, however the scenarios run in the heads of the experts, as well as in the heads of the withholders of the aids, they would have never thought of what followed.

Rwandans stood up together, again.

I remember participating in the mails on different forums, where Rwandans were wondering what to do in order to pass through those hard times, sharing thoughts.

And you know what? They found a way.

They all agreed that far from accepting to bow and agree to some nonsense, for the sake of receiving a financial aid, that would later be used as a mean to control them, they should find a solution.

They chose to stand firm.

They chose to stand with the truth, and see what would happen. And doing so, they all decided to back up their government.

A solution to this problem had to be found; there was no way Rwandans were going to wait again. History had proven that just like nobody had come to help before; nobody was going to come now.

This is when AGACIRO DEVELOPMENT FUND was born. A fund that is the first Rwandan solidarity fund, based on voluntary donations. AGACIRO is a

Kinyarwanda word that means SELF-DIGNITY, so this fund depict the dignity that Rwandans want to keep, despite all!

Anyway, Instead of waiting for the International Community to organize round table meetings, think about it, blame these or those people, decide whether or not Rwanda was liable of whatever allegations against it . . . Rwandans decided that it was enough!!!

To be disposed to continue with the planned work of sustainable development that it has undertaken since 1994, to be able to allow Rwandans to continue with their everyday life in peace, something had to be done . . . And this was done by encouraging all Rwandans to get involved.

This fund is not like some people said; nobody was forced to give up his money.

Every Rwandan, depending on what he or she earns subscribed to give a certain amount of money to the Fund in order to support the developmental work that's being done in Rwanda, to try and compensate for the Aid that was being hold off; and this was done all over the World.

In my opinion, this is the kind of support that trusted government should get from their constituents. And with such a support, a president and his government can only accomplish wonders!

It enlightened us, and we all understood that before waiting on somebody else, before waiting on external aid, it is important to try everything one can to solve one's problem—especially when this aid comes with conditions and restraints.

And if you think about it, it applies not only to Rwandans but to all third world countries, to Africans and to everyone, in every situation of everyday life.

It applies to you wherever you are; whether you are in your house, at you work, in your community or in your own country.

It taught us to be autonomous, and to take our own responsibilities!

A lesson needed by all, and long overdue!!!

Like **President Paul Kagame** says:" We cannot turn the clock back nor can we undo the harm caused, but we have the power to determine the future and to ensure that what happened never happens again".

So whether it's about an individual striving for his survival; whether it's about a group of people, getting together to strive for their survival and their offspring's; whether it's a country trying to build itself, and develop its overall social, financial and political departments . . .

Self-Reliance is a trait that is needed by everyone.

A really simple lesson to take from this is that as long as we remain dependent on others, we will always be in trouble.

Whereas the minute you start believing in your own capabilities, your own judgment, and your own resource, the minute you start believing in yourself, your life is changed for the best!!!

And this is what is happening to Rwandans right now.

This year's theme is:

2014: *"Kwibuka20: Remember, Rebuild, Renew"*

20 years later, there is hope! We strive to remember, so that our children, and their children can know what happened, and keep it from happening again. The country is being rebuilt, having in mind a prosperous future, thereby getting our nation a re-birth! Visit the country and you will be the judge of that. It is renewed, and it all have been done by Rwandans!

It's been a long run.

But "Rwanda's CEO"[4] cannot, and will not allow another failure, another bankruptcy of his

---

[4]   Rwanda Inc, written by Patricia Crisafulli and Andrea Redmond

company . . . of *our company, RWANDA.* Neither will Rwandans, neither will i!

Most Rwandans now understand the issues in play, and are ready to do their best to support their authorities, their CEO, using their knowledge, their intelligence, their skills and competencies, in order to bring only success to their company.

It's like a family business right now . . .

And like any family business, everybody is involved and everybody is ready to strive for success!

We understand that we are all in this together, at least most of us do; because I can assure you, the consequences of any fall outs will definitely ruin us all!

Whether it's through an active participation, or a passive but watchful participation, Rwandans wherever they are, they all should have the best wishes for this "company" they share.

Everyone should have this wish regardless of his personal vendetta! For it would be a pity to watch Rwanda fall back again!

So I join in and say: NEVER AGAIN!

REFERENCES

- My childhood real stories
- Culture and customs of Rwandans
- Ibuka archives
- Unity and Reconciliation courses
- http://www.gov.rw/
- The New times archives
- Rwanda Inc, written by Patricia Crisafulli and Andrea Redmond
- Encyclopedia of Africa
- Shake hands with the Devil: The failure of humanity in Rwanda, by Dallaire, Romeo (2005)

AKNOWLEDGEMENT

My thanks to Alice, Françoise, Clarisse, Benjamin, Fabrice, Espérance, Stephane, Fabrice, Doris, Peace, my nieces and nephews, Rose, to all family and friends who have been there for me in many ways. Your constant presence in my life, your love and support keeps me going.

To my mother; in addition to giving me life, you have been my model, my confident, my rock, and my all. The values of life passed on to me by you and dad will always guide me! You have been a mother to me and to my kids, and I shall be indebted to you for the rest of my life. I love you eternally!

Special thanks to my daughters Teta Charlize and Sena Estrella, you are my inspiration and my life's purpose. Your sacrifice, your encouragements, your love and support even though you are now too young to comprehend are too precious to me. My heart beats for you, and I am proud and lucky to have you!

To, Hugues, Claude, François, to everyone who motivated me, encouraged me, participated and supported this project during the whole time I was writing; it is not the words that makes a book, but the people who surrounds and inspire us.

To Mike the proofreader who stayed, to the whole team at Author House; you made self-publishing seem not so lonely. Your support was highly appreciated!

"Time and again these past twenty years, Rwandans have given of themselves. Your sacrifices are a gift to the nation. They are the seed from which the new Rwanda grows. I say to Rwandans—let's not get diverted. Our approach is as radical and unprecedented as the situation we faced. There is more hard work ahead of us than behind us. But Rwandans are ready"

—President Kagame addressing thousands gathered at Amahoro Stadium for 20th Commemoration of the Genocide Against the Tutsi.

ABOUT THE AUTHOR

Rwandan born and raised in exile, single mother of 2 beautiful little girls, Francine holds a biomedical engineering degree and is currently doing an MBA + Masters in Health Management program at Clark University while working in Poland . Being one of the founders and currently president of the Rwandan Diaspora in Poland association, she is a patriot who works towards the emphasis that everyone should have a place, a country to call home.

She writes articles, blogs and books to share her lifetimes' tragedies, opinions and experiences with her kids and everyone out there. Her hobbies include reading, photography, culture, exotic cuisine, and volunteering. She likes to occupy herself with researching about medical informatics and technologies, projects/events innovation and management. She practices swimming as a way to stay fit.

She's been living between Poland and France for the last 5 years, travelling for work in Europe and Africa, but her family still lives in Kigali-Rwanda since 2012 where her permanent home is; she visits them as often as she can.

Printed in the United States
By Bookmasters